More Praise for *The Sexy Vegan's Happy Hour at Home*

"While courting his future wife, Patton (a chef by trade) prepared a to-die-for spread of cocktails and appetizers for the couple to enjoy every Friday night. Friends started joining in the fun, and now many of the recipes from these festive gatherings can be yours....Want to wow your beloved? Let Brian's Yamburger Sliders and Rigatoni Poppers get the job done."

— **Colleen Holland, VegNews.com**

"I've never had so much fun using a cookbook as I did with *The Sexy Vegan's Happy Hour at Home*! With his creative recipes, kitchen tips, drink pairings, and premade shopping lists, Brian Patton provides everything needed to dazzle friends with the perfect vegan happy hour. *Happy Hour at Home* is more than just a cookbook, it's a recipe for a good time."

— **Quarrygirl, quarrygirl.com**

"Brian Patton is crazy, but he's the fun kind of crazy, the kind of crazy person that you want to go to a party with, and when you wake up in the morning you can't believe how much fun you had and that you didn't get arrested. *The Sexy Vegan's Happy Hour at Home* is a glimpse into the crazy that is Brian Patton. The recipes are delicious and fun to make, and they wouldn't be Brian Patton recipes if they weren't also funny. Bring *Happy Hour at Home* home with you. You won't regret it."

— **Sarah Kramer, coauthor of *How It All Vegan!***

Praise for *The Sexy Vegan Cookbook* by Brian L. Patton

"This decidedly unpreachy vegan collection comes from the founder of thesexyvegan.com and creator of vegan cooking instruction vi
have become YouTube sensations....It's a really funny book, w
something most cookbooks — especially not most vegan co
— can claim. Recipes are simple and approachable, and they
erything....The author demystifies ingredients with 'WTF is....
and many recipes feature smartphone scan codes that lead re

a relevant cooking video — a nice interactive touch in this fresh, of-the-moment volume."

— ***Publishers Weekly***

"Anyone who starts out a cookbook with a quote from Mr. Spock is already a winner in our (cook)book. *The Sexy Vegan* isn't short on anything: humor, sass, creativity, or delicious food. We're particularly excited about Patton's breakfast chapter aptly titled 'The Second Most Important Meal of the Day, After Cocktails.' Humor and the Mostest Ultimate-est Breakfast Sandwich in the History of the Universe? We're in love."

— **VegNews.com**

"More irreverent than sexy, this new vegan cookbook puts a zesty spin on traditionally meat-centric dishes, such as burgers, sliders, and ribs."

— ***Library Journal***

"Reserve a spot on your bookshelf for this one. It's a must-have!"

— **Ed Begley, Jr., actor, activist, and author of *Living Like Ed: A Guide to the Eco-Friendly Life***

"Brian Patton takes the mystery out of cooking with easy-to-find ingredients and simple presentation. And with sexy offerings like the Portly Fellow, Bourbon Tempeh Sliders, and Buffalo Wangs, this is the perfect book for the veg-curious or the veg-committed."

— **Rory Freedman, coauthor of *Skinny Bitch***

"Jam-packed with unfussy yet inventive recipes that anyone can make. The perfect starting point for dudes (and dudettes) with minimal cooking skills, and quite possibly the most-fun-to-browse vegan cookbook ever."

— **Vegan.com**

THE SEXY VEGAN'S HAPPY HOUR — AT HOME —

Also by Brian L. Patton

The Sexy Vegan Cookbook:
Extraordinary Food from an Ordinary Dude

THE SEXY VEGAN'S HAPPY HOUR — AT — HOME

SMALL PLATES, BIG FLAVORS & POTENT COCKTAILS

BRIAN L. PATTON

New World Library
Novato, California

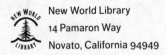

New World Library
14 Pamaron Way
Novato, California 94949

Text design by Tracy Cunningham

Photos on pages 84 and 160 by Brian L. Patton; photos on pages 15, 43, 74, 80, 87, 100, 184, and of shopping cart with all shopping lists courtesy of Bigstock. All other photos by Dan Boissy.

Library of Congress Cataloging-in-Publication Data
Patton, Brian L., date.
The sexy vegan's happy hour at home : small plates, big flavors, and potent cocktails / Brian L. Patton.
pages cm
Includes index.
ISBN 978-1-60868-234-8 (pbk.) — ISBN 978-1-60868-203-4 (ebook)
1. Vegan cooking. I. Title. II. Title: Happy hour at home.
TX837.P343 2013
641.5'636—dc23 2013005170

First printing, June 2013
ISBN 978-1-60868-234-8
Printed in Canada on 100% postconsumer-waste recycled paper

New World Library is proud to be a Gold Certified Environmentally Responsible Publisher. Publisher certification awarded by Green Press Initiative.
www.greenpressinitiative.org

10 9 8 7 6 5 4 3 2 1

"Cooking for people is an enormously significant expression of generosity and soulfulness, and entertaining is a way to be both generous and creative. You're sharing your life with people. Of course, it's also an expression of your own need for approval and applause. Nothing wrong with that."

— Ted Allen

Contents

Introduction

HELLO, PEOPLE! SEXY VEGAN HERE...AGAIN. Yes, this is my second cookbook. Yes, it is both fun and delicious. And yes (as I do the old Jedi-mind-trick two-finger wave), you *are* going to love it. Whether or not you were wondering how this book came to be, I'm about to tell you. I was sitting at my computer one day and got an email from the editor at New World Library. As I remember it, she said something to the effect of, "Your first book is selling really well, and we project that it will continue to sell, and we love you better than all our other authors, and you're the best at everything. Oh, and do you have any ideas for another book?"

And I said something to the effect of, "Absolutely! I have many, many ideas for another cookbook!" So then I went and quickly made up a bunch of ideas for another cookbook and sent them to her. She wasn't so into *The Great Sexy Caper* or *Sexy Takes Manhattan*. Also quickly shot down were *Indiana Sexy and the Tempeh of Doom*, *Pie Hard*, and *Toastbusters*. I guess the audience for *Toastbusters* would've been a bit narrow...so *that*, I get. What I didn't get was the pure disdain she had for my all-Indian cookbook, *Sexy 2: Electric Vindaloo*. I think people would've bought that one! Oh well. Of the quickly made-up ideas, *Happy Hour at Home* was one that was based on actual events, instead of being based on my dumb childhood, of which I can't seem to let go. So we went with that one.

In the summer of 2011, I accidentally started a little tradition for me and the Girlfriend, who, in the meantime, became the Fiancée, and is now the Wife — sorry ladies, I'm off the market...mostly...okay, okay, completely. I usually get home from work about an hour before she does and make dinner...and then clean the kitchen...and then take out the trash...and then fix shit with tools. Yes, I'm a dreamboat. Moving on. One Friday I didn't have enough stuff in the fridge to make a proper meal, and with the mortal fear of the wrath of a hungry girlfriend coming home to no dinner on the table, I desperately raided the pantry, freezer, and every nook and cranny of the fridge. A can of beans here, some sun-dried tomatoes there, some frozen corn, a half a jalapeño pepper, assorted olives, and pita chips. With a few flicks of the wrist and a couple spins of the blender blade, BLAM!, I had a white-bean-and-sun-dried-tomato dip with pita chips, a bowl of olives, and a quick jalapeño corn chowder. Thus, *Happy Hour at Home* was born...and more important, I didn't have to sleep on the couch.

I continued to do this "tapas" thing every Friday. I'd make up two or three simple little dishes and serve them with mixed olives or nuts and, of course, some adult beverages. I got a nice cocktail table with high stools to put on the balcony and hung some little lights above it. We'd eat, drink, enjoy the clouds painted in hues of pink and orange by the setting sun, and make fun of the people on the street below as we watched them parallel-park poorly...romance at its finest.

I still dream of making big rectangular signs to hold up, with the numbers 1 through 10 on them, and becoming the Parallel Parking Judge from atop my lofty perch. I'll do it one day. There will be so many factors to judge upon. Level of difficulty will be determined by a ratio of size of car to size of parking space. Then you can judge on approach, number of moves, and total time elapsed. Once the car is in the spot, you then judge on the FCD (final curb distance), the AVD (adjacent vehicle distance), and, of course, parallelityness (a word I just made up). Naturally, there will be deductions for contact with any curbs or AVs, and if a friend has to get out of the car to coach the driver, I will hit the big buzzer and a trapdoor will open, swallowing the contestant and his or her car. Hey, major networks, consider this my official pitch for the next great competition show. I'd like to have Howard Stern and Carmen Electra on the judging panel as well. Thank you.

Holy tangent, Batman! Didn't see that one coming. So what was I talking about? Oh yeah. Happy hour. The intimate, romantic aspect of these little dinners, however, did not last long. As word got out about our happy hour at home (and by "word got out" I mean the Girlfriend bragging to all her friends), people started wondering when they would get an invitation. Since we can accommodate only four people on the balcony (happy hour *must* take place on the balcony, as you'll see in the following "rules" section), we had to start taking reservations — from our friends. Fridays started to get booked up, and what was once a casual weekly meal became a job...a job for ME!! Everyone else got to relax and have a good time, while I slaved away! Alas, 'tis the life I've chosen.

So I figured I'd start taking happy hour seriously and plan out menus to wow my diners. They weren't allowed to know in advance what was being served, and I even went so far as to install a chalkboard in my kitchen, where I would post the menu. However, because I like to tease my guests, I wouldn't write the menu on the chalkboard until about 10 minutes before serving. It was part of the experience.

Once summer ended and darkness began creeping in earlier and earlier, I decided that "happy hour season" was over and would not return until I declared its beginning sometime in spring. I lifted this idea from my college buddy, the Great TLP, who would declare the beginning of "rum season" every spring. When he determined that the cold days were behind us (we were in Pennsylvania), he would put the stereo speakers in the window of our fraternity house, sit on the back porch with a rum and Coke, and blast Jimmy Buffett. Then and only then did rum season begin…like we needed another excuse to drink.

So, anyway, I use similar criteria for determining the open and close of "happy hour season." Speaking of criteria, I have established the following rules for happy hour in my home. You, of course, can use these, make up your own, or have complete anarchy and chaos.

1. Happy hour is always served on the balcony.
2. Happy hour season may begin only when the weather is such that once the sun goes down, even the whiniest of guests won't get chilly sitting outside, because, see rule no. 1.
3. Happy hour is on Friday. Period.
4. Happy hour is for four people. Any more, and

you'd have a dinner party, and that'd be a different book.

5. Happy hour guests may not be made privy to the menu until the chef posts it. Chalkboards optional but encouraged.
6. Guests bring the booze, at the chef's instruction.

And finally...

7. There's no crying in happy hour.

With the rules laid out, you are now ready to conduct your own happy hour. But I want to tell you a few things about this book before you begin:

The book is segmented into menus instead of chapters. The menus are themed, and each one's dishes are designed to go together, as you'll see. Also, each menu in the book serves four people. So don't look through it and whine, "Wah, how many servings does this make? It doesn't say!" The answer is four. Every recipe is for four.

These menus are designed to be prepared in about an hour. I really wanted to make them efficient, so I offer you the option of taking shortcuts and using some store-bought items. For example, instead of making my Basic Pizza Dough, Pretend Italian Sausages, and Tempeh Chorizo from scratch, you can buy packaged versions (like ready-made dough, Tofurky or Field Roast sausages, and Soyrizo), which I encourage you to use, in order to cut down on happy hour prep time. I showed you how to make these items in my first book, which you already own: *The Sexy Vegan Cookbook: Extraordinary Food from an Ordinary Dude*. So I don't want to see any goddamn online reviews saying, "Oh, he uses store-bought stuff." I already showed you how to make dat shit! I'm just trying to save you time here, you bastiges! However, if you insist on making everything from scratch, you don't have to disassemble the shrine on your mantle where my first book resides — I've provided the optional recipes in their entirety here as well. You're welcome.

I have also added efficiency tips, which help you do things in a manner that uses your time in the kitchen most wisely. Many people who are bad cooks are bad not because they don't have the knowledge or palate but because they don't know how to manage their time in the kitchen. I hope to shed some light on that subject with the efficiency tips.

I've put together a gallery of color photos of some of the dishes presented in this book. Scan this QR code to check it out.

Scan to view the gallery.
http://www.thesexyvegan.com/gallery

You'll find other QR codes sprinkled throughout the book, and they link to helpful videos of me demonstrating select recipes. I'll periodically update the links to offer bonus recipes and tips, so be sure to follow, like, and subscribe to the Sexy Vegan at my various social media outlets to keep yourself informed of the updates.

www.thesexyvegan.com
www.facebook.com/thesexyvegan
www.twitter.com/thesexyvegan
www.youtube.com/lukin82

At the end of each menu you'll find a handy-dandy shopping list. The shopping lists include every ingredient you will need to prepare the recipes, including staples you might already have on hand, like olive oil, salt, and pepper. Obviously, you don't need to buy more of something you already have just because it's on the shopping list. And if one dish calls for ½ bell pepper, sliced, and another dish in the same menu calls for ½ bell pepper, diced, the menu's shopping list will tell you to buy only one bell pepper. Also, in some cases the amounts I have given in the shopping lists reflect what you'll find in the store. So the shopping list might say "Tarragon (1 bunch)" or "Yellow onion (1)" even though the related recipe only calls for ½ cup chopped fresh tarragon or ½ yellow onion. I trust that you'll find some creative way to use up the excess ingredients.

Finally — and some might think most important — in the introduction to each menu, I suggest an adult beverage to serve with the dishes. Some of those beverages are specialty cocktails that I have created for this book, and the recipes for those cocktails are gathered in the last chapter.

I think that's about it. Get your reservation book out, because your house is about to be the most popular joint in town. Let's get happy!

1 HOLY STROMBOLI

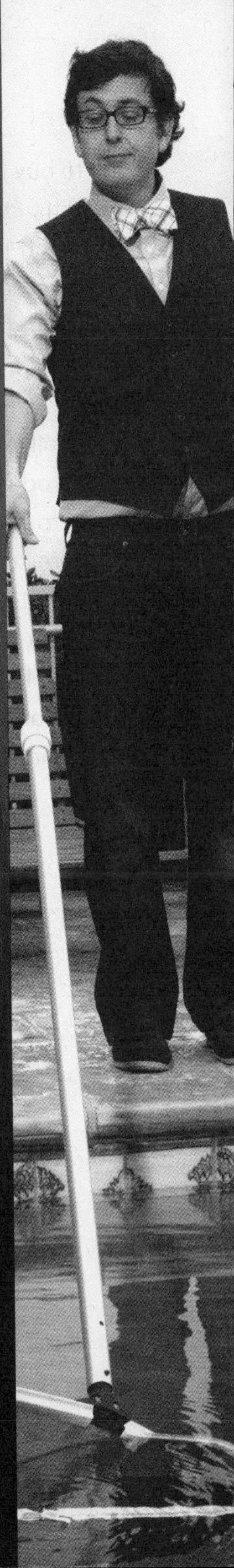

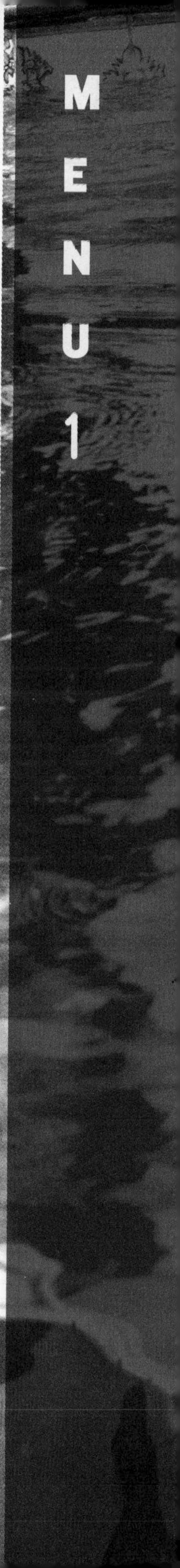

Up until I became a vegan, stromboli was an integral part of my life. When it was dinnertime in my house, we had the choice of pizza, stromboli, pizza, or pizza, and that was about it. A stromboli is essentially a tube of pizza, or an elongated calzone, and serves about four to six people — or one fat twelve-year-old. A stromboli is usually filled with ham, salami, pepperoni, peppers, onions, and cheese.

In college I had the (un)fortunate situation of living right next door to a pizza place. Lunch usually consisted of a Rico Boli (a mini stromboli, with basically one of every animal in it), garlic cheese bread, and an order of dough fritz (fried dough topped with powdered sugar). In fact, my nickname became Dough Fritz — sometimes shortened to Dough, or Fritz. What a life I had carved out for myself! How I made it out of there alive, I'll never know.

So you may know the glory that is stromboli, I have created a vegan version.

LIBATION RECOMMENDATION

To accompany this delicacy, just grab whatever floaters of shitty light beer are left on your coffee table from the night before — and make sure there are no cigarette butts floating in the cup. If you didn't happen to throw a rager in your living room the night before, however, try accompanying your stromboli with a Starburst (see recipe, page 201), as I did many times back in the day.

EFFICIENCY TIP

The cannoli filling and the giardiniera will hold in the refrigerator for a few days, so you can make those ahead of time.

Stromboli

2 teaspoons extra-virgin olive oil, plus more for brushing
½ red bell pepper, sliced
½ medium yellow onion, sliced
¼ teaspoon dried oregano
¼ teaspoon dried basil
Salt
¼ pound button or cremini mushrooms, sliced
2 cups bite-size broccoli florets
Pepper
Unbleached all-purpose flour for dusting the work surface
1 pound store-bought pizza dough or Basic Pizza Dough (recipe follows), at room temperature
8 ounces mozzarella-style vegan cheeze, shredded
¼ cup sliced pitted black or kalamata olives
2 cups marinara sauce, warmed

Scan to watch the video.

Preheat your pizza stone on the middle rack of your oven for 1 hour at 400°F. Yeah, you have to — just open your windows and stop whining about the heat.

In a large skillet, heat 2 teaspoons oil over medium heat. Add the bell pepper, onion, oregano, basil, and a pinch of salt. Cook for 3 minutes, then add the mushrooms. Cook for 3 to 4 more minutes, until the mushrooms are tender, then add the broccoli. Once the broccoli is tender, about 4 more minutes, season the veggies with salt and pepper to taste. Transfer the veggies to a bowl and let cool.

On a floured surface, roll the pizza dough into an oval that is approximately 13 to 14 inches long and 9 to 10 inches wide. Transfer the dough to a floured pizza peel — one of those giant spatulas they use to put the pizzas in the oven at pizzerias. You have one, remember? I told you to buy one in my first book; therefore, you did.

Fold the mozzarella and olives into the bowl of veggies — this is your filling. Place the filling in an elongated pile in the middle of the dough, making sure that there are 2 to 3 inches between the edges of the dough and the filling on all sides. Fold in the short sides of the dough so that they cover a couple inches of the filling. Then take one long side of the dough and fold it in half so that the long sides meet, completely covering the filling. Pinch the edges of the dough together.

With a paring knife, make three 1-inch slits in the top of the stromboli to release steam. Brush the top of the stromboli with a generous amount of olive oil. At this point the dough might be sticking to the peel, so gently run your hands under the stromboli to make sure it's not sticking. Just before transferring the stromboli to the pizza stone, give it a little shimmy shake to make sure it will slide off. Then with one easy motion, thrust the peel forward over the stone, then quickly pull back to let the stromboli slide off.

Bake for 15 to 17 minutes, until the top is browned and crisp. Let cool for 5 minutes, then cut crosswise into 4 pieces. Serve with the warmed marinara.

BASIC PIZZA DOUGH

1 cup warm water

One 7-gram package or 2¼ teaspoons active dry yeast

1 tablespoon extra-virgin olive oil, plus more to coat the dough and bowl

1 tablespoon agave nectar

Healthy pinch of salt

3 cups unbleached all-purpose flour, plus more for dusting the work surface

In a bowl, combine the water, yeast, 1 tablespoon oil, agave nectar, and salt. Gently mix it all together and let it sit for 5 minutes, until it starts to froth. This ensures the yeast is active and has not expired. Add 2 cups of the flour and mix it up (I do it by hand, but you could use a stand mixer with a dough hook). Continue to slowly add the rest of the flour until you have a slightly sticky ball. Then knead the dough by hand or in your stand mixer. You can add a little flour if the dough starts to stick to your hands. You'll need to knead the dough until it is smooth and elastic; this will take about 10 minutes by hand (or 5 minutes on medium speed if you're using a stand mixer). After kneading, form it into a ball.

Coat a large bowl with olive oil. (The dough is going to double in size in that bowl, so make sure the bowl is big enough.) Also coat the dough in olive oil. Put the dough in the bowl, cover it with a damp kitchen towel, and stash it someplace warm for 90 minutes for its first rise. I find that turning my oven on to 200°F for 2 minutes, then turning it off, creates the perfect environment for rising dough. After the first rise, give the dough a couple of light, open-handed slaps to make it collapse so that it's flattened out. Then let it rise for 40 more minutes.

Now your dough is ready to use and is the equivalent of 1 pound of store-bought dough.

Quick Giardiniera

3 cups distilled white vinegar

3 cups water

3 tablespoons unrefined granulated sugar

1 bay leaf

½ teaspoon chile flakes

½ teaspoon salt, plus more as needed

1 small head cauliflower, trimmed and cut into bite-size florets

2 stalks celery, thinly sliced

1 carrot, thinly sliced

1 red bell pepper, cut into 1-inch chunks

3 tablespoons extra-virgin olive oil

Pepper

In a saucepan, combine the vinegar, water, sugar, bay leaf, chile flakes, and ½ teaspoon salt, and bring to a boil over high heat, stirring to help dissolve the sugar. Once the sugar is dissolved, add the cauliflower, celery, carrot, and bell pepper. Reduce the heat to medium and simmer for 3 minutes, until the veggies are tender-crisp. Remove the pot from the heat and let rest at room temperature for at least an hour, or until the veggies have cooled.

Drain the vegetables, reserving 3 tablespoons of the cooking liquid. Transfer the vegetables to a medium bowl, and toss with the oil and the reserved cooking liquid. Season with salt and pepper to taste. Refrigerate until party time, then serve cold or at room temperature.

Cannoli Cups

½ cup whole raw cashews, soaked overnight, or boiled for 10 minutes and drained
4 ounces vegan cream cheeze
½ teaspoon white wine
2 tablespoons powdered sugar, plus more for dusting
Pinch of salt
12 vegan phyllo dough cups (see WTF below)
12 raspberries

In a food processor or blender, process the cashews until finely ground. Add the cream cheeze, white wine, powdered sugar, and salt, and process until smooth. Spoon the filling into the phyllo cups, and top each one with a raspberry. Dust with powdered sugar. Serve chilled or at room temperature.

WTF are vegan phyllo dough cups? Phyllo is a flaky pastry dough sold in very thin sheets. Most times it is vegan, but be sure to check the list of ingredients. You can find the preformed, prebaked cups of which I speak in the freezer section of most supermarkets.

SHOPPING LIST

Holy Stromboli

PRODUCE

Raspberries (1/2 pint)
Red bell peppers (2)
Broccoli (1 bunch)
Carrot (1)
Cauliflower (1 small head)
Celery (2 stalks)
Button or cremini mushrooms (1/4 pound)
Yellow onion (1 medium)

PANTRY

Unbleached all-purpose flour (for dusting the work surface)
Powdered sugar (2 tablespoons)
Unrefined granulated sugar (3 tablespoons)
Marinara sauce (16 fluid ounces [2 cups])
Extra-virgin olive oil (about 1/4 cup)
Distilled white vinegar (24 fluid ounces [3 cups])
Cashews, whole raw (1/2 cup)
Black or kalamata olives, pitted (about 1/3 cup)
Dried basil (1/4 teaspoon)
Bay leaf (1)
Chile flakes (1/2 teaspoon)
Dried oregano (1/4 teaspoon)
Salt
Pepper

MISCELLANEOUS

White wine (1/2 teaspoon)
Mozzarella-style vegan cheeze (8 ounces)
Vegan cream cheeze (4 ounces)
Vegan phyllo dough cups (12)
Pizza dough (1 pound) — OR if you want to make my Basic Pizza Dough, you'll need:
- Unbleached all-purpose flour (3 cups, plus more for dusting the work surface)
- Active dry yeast (one 7-gram package or 2 1/4 teaspoons)
- Agave nectar (1 tablespoon)
- Extra-virgin olive oil (about 2 tablespoons)

2

BE STILL, MY HEARTS OF PALM

Hearts of Palm Ceviche

Mango Gazpacho

Chile-Cilantro Garlic Bread

Shopping List

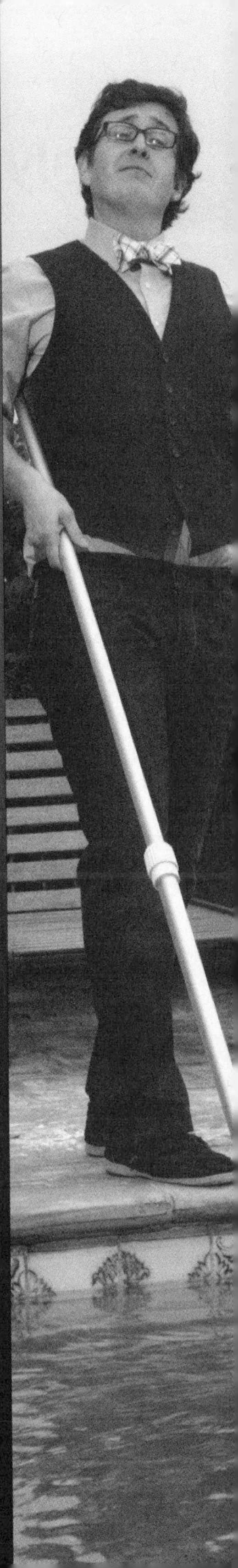

Look, I know that ceviche is South American and gazpacho is Spanish, but they taste good together, okay?! And if you don't like mixing regions on your menu, then you're really not going to like the beverage I'm about to recommend....

LIBATION RECOMMENDATION

Witbier. A Belgian-style beer infused with orange peel and coriander, it goes great with the cilantro and citrus in these dishes. The Solid Gold (see recipe, page 205) would also be a great choice, or since you're already working with mangoes, whip up a batch of the Mangled Mango (see recipe, page 198).

EFFICIENCY TIP

The longer the ceviche marinates, the better it will be. Ideally, put it together in the morning so that it's ready by happy hour — which also means you'll have one less thing to do in the afternoon. If you've got the time, you can even make the gazpacho in the morning as well. It comes together quickly, and the extra time will give the flavors a chance to marry. The garlic bread takes almost no time at all, so make that just before serving.

Hearts of Palm Ceviche

One 14-ounce can hearts of palm, rinsed and cut into bite-size pieces
1 jalapeño pepper
4 ounces cherry tomatoes, halved
½ garlic clove, grated
¼ cup fresh lime juice
¼ cup fresh orange juice
2 tablespoons extra-virgin olive oil
1 tablespoon roughly chopped fresh cilantro
1 scallion, thinly sliced
¼ teaspoon salt
½ avocado
Pepper
Tortilla chips

Slice the jalapeño pepper into 8 thin slices. Reserve the stem end of the pepper for use in the Chile-Cilantro Garlic Bread (see recipe, page 24). Place the hearts of palm, jalapeño pepper, cherry tomatoes, garlic, lime juice, orange juice, oil, cilantro, scallion, and ¼ teaspoon salt in a large zip-top bag. Slosh the ingredients around until they are combined. Squeeze the bag to suck out as much of the air as possible, and zip it closed. Put the bag in the fridge to let the ceviche marinate for at least 1 hour.

Just before serving, transfer the ceviche to a large bowl. Dice the avocado, add it to the bowl, and gently toss it with the ceviche. Season with salt and pepper to taste. Serve with tortilla chips.

Mango Gazpacho

2 mangoes, peeled and cubed (about 3 cups)
⅓ English cucumber, peeled and roughly chopped (about 1 cup)
½ red bell pepper, roughly chopped
⅓ cup roughly chopped red onion
¼ jalapeño pepper, seeded
½ garlic clove
¼ cup fresh orange juice
½-inch piece fresh ginger, peeled and grated
1 tablespoon roughly chopped fresh cilantro, plus 4 sprigs for garnish
Salt and pepper

A blender would work best for this but a food processor will do too. In your blending device, combine the mangoes, cucumber, bell pepper, onion, jalapeño pepper, garlic, orange juice, ginger, and chopped cilantro, and puree until smooth. Season with salt and pepper to taste. Chill for at least 1 hour. Transfer to 4 individual bowls, and garnish each bowl with a cilantro sprig.

Chile-Cilantro Garlic Bread

½ baguette, halved lengthwise

¼ cup vegan margarine

¼ teaspoon ancho chile powder, plus more for garnish

Pinch of salt

1 large garlic clove, halved crosswise

Jalapeño pepper end, reserved from the Hearts of Palm Ceviche (see recipe, page 22)

2 tablespoons finely chopped fresh cilantro

Set your broiler on high. Slather both baguette halves with margarine, and dust with ¼ teaspoon chile powder and the salt. Place the baguette halves, cut sides up, under the broiler for 30 seconds to 1 minute, or until browned around the edges. Remove the baguette halves from the broiler, and immediately rub with the cut sides of the garlic and the jalapeño pepper. Garnish with the cilantro and a pinch of chile powder. Cut each baguette half into 4 pieces.

Be Still, My Hearts of Palm

PRODUCE

Mangoes (2)
Limes (2)
Cherry tomatoes (½ pint)
Avocado (1)
Jalapeño peppers (2)
Red bell pepper (1)
English cucumber (1)
Scallions (1 bunch)
Red onion (1 medium)
Garlic (2 cloves)
Ginger (one ½-inch piece)
Cilantro (1 bunch)

PANTRY

Hearts of palm (one 14-ounce can)
Extra-virgin olive oil (2 tablespoons)
Ancho chile powder (¼ teaspoon, plus a pinch for garnish)
Salt
Pepper

MISCELLANEOUS

Fresh orange juice (½ cup)
Vegan margarine (¼ cup)
Baguette
Tortilla chips

3

Polenta Party

Creamy Polenta

Pretend Italian Sausages and Peppers

Mixed Mushrooms

Tender Green Cabbage

Shopping List

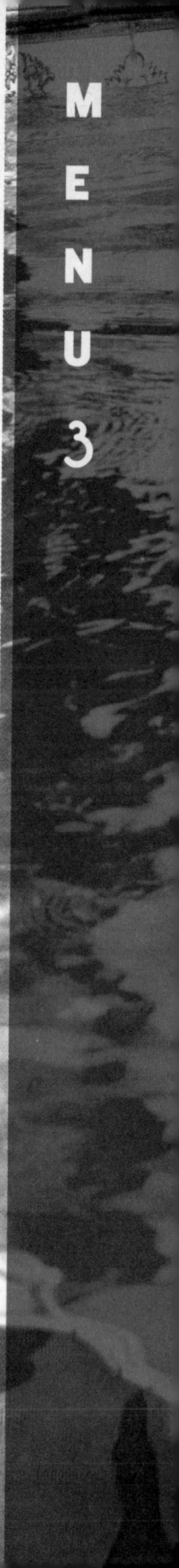

Who doesn't think "party" when they hear the word *polenta*? I know I don't not...I think. Now, I know you're looking at the Green Cabbage recipe and thinking, "Cabbage? Just plain cabbage?" Yes. When prepared simply, cabbage is really tender and sweet, just like Jon from *The Real World 2*. Green Cabbage is a perfect complement to the Pretend Italian Sausages and Peppers and the Mixed Mushrooms, as I imagine Jon from *The Real World 2* would also be.

LIBATION RECOMMENDATION

You definitely want wine for this menu, and since there's red wine in one dish and white wine in the other, you've already got two open bottles, so drink 'em both. For reds, I usually prefer a cabernet, and for whites, I go with sauvignon blanc. Here's a related question: Is it bad that as soon as I open a bottle of wine for myself, I automatically throw the cork away?

EFFICIENCY TIP

The Green Cabbage, Pretend Italian Sausages and Peppers, and Mixed Mushrooms can be made a day ahead of time, if you like, and then reheated on the stove just before serving. You should make the polenta just before you're ready to serve.

Creamy Polenta

4 cups water

¼ teaspoon salt, plus more as needed

1 cup cornmeal

2 tablespoons vegan margarine

1 tablespoon nutritional yeast

1 garlic clove, grated

Pepper

1 tablespoon finely chopped fresh Italian parsley

In a medium pot, bring the water to a rolling boil over high heat. Add 1 teaspoon salt and begin whisking the water in a circular motion. Slowly pour the cornmeal into the boiling water in a steady stream, constantly whisking to prevent lumps. Whisk for 2 to 3 minutes, or until the polenta begins to thicken. Reduce the heat to low, and whisk in the vegan margarine, nutritional yeast, and garlic. Simmer, stirring often, for 25 minutes. The finished product should be thick, yet pourable. Season with salt and pepper to taste.

To serve, pour the hot polenta into a wide plate with high edges or a large oval serving bowl. Picture the plate divided into thirds, and mound each of the three toppings (Pretend Sausages and Peppers, Mixed Mushrooms, and Green Cabbage) onto one of the thirds. Garnish with parsley.

Pretend Italian Sausages and Peppers

3 teaspoons extra-virgin olive oil
Three 3-ounce store-bought vegan sausages or 3 Pretend Italian Sausages (recipe follows), sliced on the bias
1 red bell pepper, sliced
1 medium yellow onion, sliced
1 teaspoon dried oregano
1 teaspoon dried basil
Salt and pepper
1 cup red wine
2 cups marinara sauce

To brown the sausages, heat 1 teaspoon of the olive oil in a skillet over medium-high heat. Place the sausages in the pan, and cook for 2 to 3 minutes, until browned on one side, then flip and repeat.

Preheat the oven to 375°F. In a medium bowl, toss the bell pepper and onion with the oregano, basil, the remaining 2 teaspoons olive oil, and a healthy pinch of salt and pepper. Transfer the vegetable mixture to a small baking dish, pour in the wine, and cover. Braise in the oven for 20 minutes, then uncover and cook for 15 more minutes. Remove from the oven, stir in the marinara, and top with the sausages. Cover and cook for 15 more minutes, or until it's all warmed through.

PRETEND ITALIAN SAUSAGES

Scan to watch the video.

½ pound russet potatoes, peeled and quartered
1 cup vital wheat gluten
1 tablespoon nutritional yeast

½ teaspoon garlic powder

½ teaspoon onion powder

½ teaspoon vegetable bouillon powder

¼ teaspoon pepper

¼ teaspoon celery seeds

Pinch of dried thyme

Pinch of ground sage

¼ teaspoon chile flakes

½ teaspoon fennel seeds

1 tablespoon chickpea flour or all-purpose flour

¼ cup low-sodium tamari

¾ cup water

¼ cup diced yellow onion

3 garlic cloves, roughly chopped

1 tablespoon chopped oil-packed sun-dried tomatoes

½ cup drained and rinsed canned white beans

In a small pot, cover the potatoes with cold water and bring to a boil. Boil for 8 to 10 minutes, or until the chunks easily fall apart when you put a fork through them. Drain the potatoes well and while they're still hot, gently mash with a fork until there are no chunks left, or pass through a potato ricer. Set aside to cool.

In a large bowl, whisk together the wheat gluten, nutritional yeast, garlic powder, onion powder, bouillon powder, pepper, celery seeds, thyme, sage, chile flakes, fennel seeds, and chickpea flour. In a food processor or blender, puree the tamari, water, onion, garlic, sun-dried tomatoes, and beans. When the potatoes are cool enough to handle, add them and the bean mixture to the bowl with the dry ingredients, and mash it all together with your hands to form a soft dough, making sure there are no dry parts remaining.

Let the dough rest for 10 minutes before using. You can also wrap it in plastic and store it in the refrigerator for later use. It will last for 5 days.

Form the dough into a loaf-like shape and cut it in half. Then cut those halves in half. Finally, cut the halves of the halves into five-sixteenths...just kidding, cut them in half. Now you'll have 8 portions. Roll them into cigar-like shapes, 4 inches long and ½ inch wide. Loosely roll each portion in foil and twist the ends of the foil to seal the packets. Remember to leave some room for expansion. Using a steamer basket, steam for 1 hour. Now they're ready to be browned or grilled in a pan.

If you don't use all 8 sausages right away, store the remaining ones in an airtight container in the fridge for up to 4 days or in the freezer for up to a month.

Mixed Mushrooms

2 teaspoons extra-virgin olive oil
4 garlic cloves, minced
2 teaspoons roughly chopped fresh thyme
1½ pounds mixed mushrooms (cremini, oyster, shiitake, trumpet, etc.), roughly chopped
½ cup dry white wine
Salt and pepper
1 lemon wedge

In a large skillet, heat the oil over medium heat. Add the garlic and thyme, and cook for 2 minutes. Add the mushrooms, tossing to coat, and cook for 5 to 6 minutes, or until the mushrooms become dark and tender. Add the wine, season with salt and pepper, and cook for about 2 minutes, or until the wine is almost evaporated. When the mushrooms are plated (see Creamy Polenta, page 28), squeeze the juice from the lemon wedge over them.

Tender Green Cabbage

2 tablespoons vegan margarine

1 medium head green cabbage, roughly chopped into 1- to 2-inch chunks

Salt and pepper

1 teaspoon red wine vinegar

In a large pot, melt the margarine over medium-high heat. Add the cabbage, and season with a healthy pinch of salt and pepper. Cook, stirring often, for 4 to 5 minutes, or until the cabbage begins to wilt. Reduce the heat to medium, stir in the vinegar, and cover. Cook, stirring occasionally, for 15 minutes. Uncover and cook for about 5 minutes, or until any liquid has evaporated. Season with salt and pepper to taste.

Polenta Party

PRODUCE

- Lemon (1)
- Red bell pepper (1)
- Green cabbage (1 medium head)
- Mixed mushrooms (cremini, oyster, shiitake, trumpet, etc.) (1½ pounds)
- Yellow onion (1 medium)
- Garlic (5 cloves)
- Thyme (1 bunch)
- Italian parsley (1 bunch)

PANTRY

- Cornmeal (1 cup)
- Nutritional yeast (1 tablespoon)
- Marinara sauce (16 fluid ounces [2 cups])
- Extra-virgin olive oil (5 teaspoons)
- Red wine vinegar (1 teaspoon)
- Dried oregano (1 teaspoon)
- Dried basil (1 teaspoon)
- Salt
- Pepper

MISCELLANEOUS

- Red wine (8 fluid ounces [1 cup])
- Dry white wine (4 fluid ounces [½ cup])
- Vegan margarine (4 tablespoons)
- Vegan sausages (three 3-ounce) — OR if you want to make my Pretend Italian Sausages, you'll need:
  - Russet potatoes (½ pound)
  - Yellow onion (1 small)
  - Garlic (3 cloves)
  - Chickpea flour or all-purpose flour (1 tablespoon)
  - Vital wheat gluten (1 cup)
  - Nutritional yeast (1 tablespoon)
  - White beans (one 15-ounce can)
  - Sun-dried tomatoes, chopped oil-packed (1 tablespoon)
  - Tamari, low-sodium (¼ cup)

Vegetable bouillon powder (½ teaspoon)
Celery seeds (¼ teaspoon)
Chile flakes (¼ teaspoon)
Fennel seeds (½ teaspoon)
Garlic powder (½ teaspoon)
Onion powder (½ teaspoon)
Ground sage (just a pinch)
Dried thyme (just a pinch)

4

GODYAMMIT, THESE SLIDERS ARE HEAVENLY!

Yamburger Sliders

Green Bean Fries with Tahini Dipping Sauce

Spiced Nuts

Shopping List

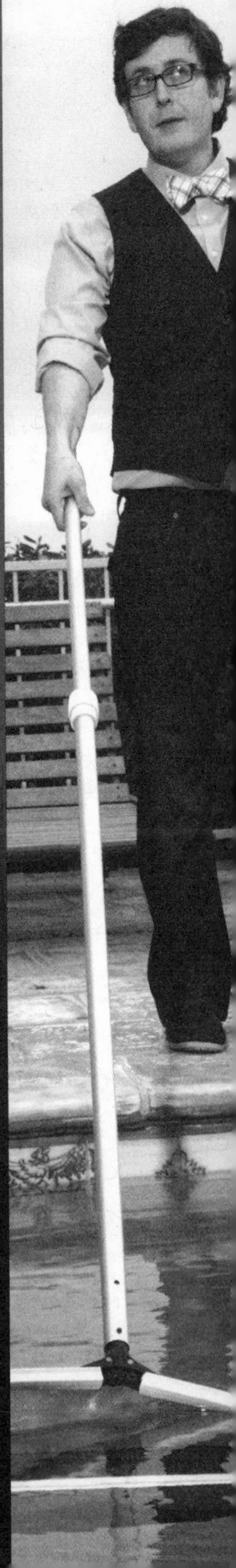

MENU 4

A slightly more healthful take on "burgers and fries," this menu is packed with a ton of flavors and spices.

LIBATION RECOMMENDATION

The Mangled Mango (see recipe, page 198) goes great with these dishes, or if fall is approaching, the warm spices and brown sugar lend themselves very well to an autumnal brew, like pumpkin ale.

EFFICIENCY TIP

Get the spiced nuts in the oven first, then work on the yam slider preparation and the tahini dressing. You can fry the yams early in your process and then keep them warm or reheat them in the oven. The fried green beans are quick and easy, so you can do them last — just make sure you have the oil heated and ready to go.

Yamburger Sliders

2 large yams, cut crosswise into twelve ½-inch-thick slices
1 heaping tablespoon brown sugar
½ teaspoon ground cumin
½ teaspoon smoked paprika
½ teaspoon ground coriander
½ teaspoon garam masala (see WTF below)
½ teaspoon salt
½ teaspoon pepper
3 teaspoons extra-virgin olive oil
12 tiny buns (about 2 inches wide), halved
Tahini Dipping Sauce (see recipe, page 42) for spreading
1 packed cup arugula
1 mango, peeled and cut into 12 very thin slices with a vegetable peeler or mandoline
12 sandwich toothpicks ("fancy" or "unfancy")

In a large pot of cold water, bring the yam slices to a boil over high heat. Boil for 6 to 7 minutes, or until the yams are just fork-tender but not too soft. Whilst your yams are boiling, in a large bowl, combine the brown sugar, cumin, paprika, coriander, garam masala, salt, pepper, and 2 teaspoons of the oil.

WTF is garam masala? It's a powerful spice mixture made primarily of pepper, cinnamon, clove, cumin, and cardamom that is used in many Indian dishes. Find it in your regular old grocery store spice aisle between the galangal and the golpar (or, as you probably know it, Persian hogweed), at an Indian market, or on the Interwebs.

Remove the yams from the pot with a slotted spoon, and cool the slices in an ice bath or under cold running water. Drain and pat dry with a paper towel. Gently toss the yam slices in the spice-and-oil mixture until they are well coated. Set aside.

Preheat the oven to 200°F. In a large skillet, heat the remaining 1 teaspoon oil over medium-high heat. Now would also be a good time to toast your tiny buns.

Working in batches, add the yam slices to the skillet and cook for 3 to 4 minutes per side, or until caramelized and slightly browned. Transfer the yams to an ovenproof plate and keep warm in the oven until you're ready to build your burgers.

Spread the bottom half of each bun with Tahini Dipping Sauce. Top with 1 yam slice, a few arugula leaves, and a slice of mango folded in half so that it fits neatly on the bun. Cover with the bun tops. Stick toothpicks through the sliders to keep them together.

Green Bean Fries with Tahini Dipping Sauce

Canola, peanut, or any other high-heat oil, for deep-frying

One 12-fluid-ounce bottle beer

1 cup unbleached all-purpose flour

½ teaspoon Sexy Sprinkle (recipe follows), plus more for dusting

½ cup arrowroot

6 ounces green beans, trimmed

Tahini Dipping Sauce (recipe follows) for dipping

Preheat the oven to 200°F. Line a plate with paper towels and set it next to the stove. Pour oil to a depth of 1½ to 2 inches in a pot, high-sided pan, or deep fryer that is wide enough to fit the longest of your green beans. Heat the oil over medium-high heat until it registers 350°F on a deep-frying thermometer.

In a large bowl, whisk together the beer, flour, and ½ teaspoon Sexy Sprinkle. Put the arrowroot in another bowl. Toss the green beans in the arrowroot until lightly coated. Working in batches, dip several of the green beans in the beer batter, allowing the excess batter to fall away.

Place the green beans directly in the hot oil, being careful not to crowd the pot. Use a slotted metal spatula or tongs to make sure that the beans don't stick to the pot bottom or to each other. Fry the green beans for 2 to 3 minutes, or until golden brown. Using a spatula or tongs, transfer the green beans to the paper towel–lined plate. Dust them immediately with a liberal amount of the Sexy Sprinkle, and keep warm in the oven.

Fry the remaining green beans in the same way, allowing the oil to return to 350°F before each batch. Serve on a platter, or in one of those cool french fry–cone things, with the Tahini Dipping Sauce on the side.

THE SEXY SPRINKLE

1 teaspoon granulated garlic or garlic powder

1 teaspoon granulated onion or onion powder

1 teaspoon smoked paprika

½ teaspoon pepper

1 teaspoon unrefined granulated sugar

½ teaspoon nutritional yeast

1 teaspoon salt

Whisk all the ingredients together until combined. If you don't use all the sprinkle right away, store the remainder in an airtight container for later use.

TAHINI DIPPING SAUCE

⅔ cup tahini

2 garlic cloves

4 teaspoons fresh lime juice

½ cup roughly chopped fresh tarragon

1 cup water

2 teaspoons agave nectar

Pinch of cayenne pepper

Salt and black pepper

In a food processor or blender, process the tahini, garlic, lime juice, tarragon, water, agave nectar, and cayenne pepper until smooth. Add more water, if needed, to achieve your desired consistency.

Season with salt and black pepper to taste. In addition to dipping your Green Bean Fries in it, use this sauce to smear all over the tiny buns for the Yamburger Sliders (see recipe, page 38).

Spiced Nuts

¼ pound whole raw almonds
¼ pound whole raw cashews
1 teaspoon extra-virgin olive oil
½ teaspoon fresh lime juice
1 teaspoon brown sugar
½ teaspoon salt
¼ teaspoon garam masala
⅛ teaspoon smoked paprika

Preheat the oven to 250°F. Line a baking sheet with parchment paper or a Silpat baking mat. In a medium bowl, combine all the ingredients and toss until the nuts are coated. Spread out the nuts in a single layer on the baking sheet. Roast for 20 minutes, then toss, and roast for 20 more minutes. Remove from the oven and let cool.

Godyammit, These Sliders Are Heavenly!

PRODUCE

Mango (1)
Limes (1)
Yams (2 large)
Arugula (1 packed cup)
Green beans (6 ounces)
Garlic (2 cloves)
Tarragon (1 bunch)

PANTRY

Unbleached all-purpose flour (1 cup)
Brown sugar (1 heaping tablespoon plus 1 teaspoon)
Unrefined granulated sugar (1 teaspoon)
Arrowroot (½ cup)
Nutritional yeast (½ teaspoon)
Agave nectar (2 teaspoons)
Extra-virgin olive oil (4 teaspoons)
Canola, peanut, or any other high-heat oil (1 or 2 quarts, depending on the size of your deep-frying vessel)
Tahini (⅔ cup)
Almonds, whole raw (¼ pound)
Cashews, whole raw (¼ pound)
Cayenne pepper (just a pinch)
Ground coriander (½ teaspoon)
Ground cumin (½ teaspoon)
Garam masala (¾ teaspoon)
Granulated garlic or garlic powder (1 teaspoon)
Granulated onion or onion powder (1 teaspoon)
Smoked paprika (1⅝ teaspoon)
Salt
Pepper

MISCELLANEOUS

Beer (one 12-fluid-ounce bottle)
Sandwich toothpicks ("fancy" or "unfancy") (12)
Tiny buns (about 2 inches wide) (12)

5

NOTHING RHYMES WITH CITRUS

Tofu-Citrus "Titrus" Dippers

Citrus Soba

Grilled Pineapple Salad

Shopping List

It's true! I couldn't find a damn thing to cleverly rhyme with *citrus*, except for words I made up, like *blitrus* and *titrus*. Ha! *Titrus*...I like that one. I'll have to think of how to use that word.

LIBATION RECOMMENDATION

The Punchy Pineapple (see recipe, page 191) was made for this menu, so, obviously, I highly recommend it. The Solid Gold (see recipe, page 205) would also complement these dishes beautifully. If you're not feeling cocktail-y, a hefeweizen would be very nice with the citrus in the tofu marinade and the soba dressing.

EFFICIENCY TIP

If you're a plan-aheader, you can drain and begin marinating the tofu in the morning, or even the day before, and it will be packed with flavor once happy hour rolls around. You want to get as much water as possible out of that block of tofu before marinating it. Remove it from the package and discard the packing water. Place the tofu on a plate, and place another plate on top of that. Then put a can or two of beans or some other canned good on the top plate to weigh it down. Let it sit like this for at least thirty minutes and up to an hour. This will press out all that pesky water, thus leaving room inside your tofu for the zingy marinade.

Tofu-Citrus "Titrus" Dippers

Citrus Marinade

½ cup orange marmalade
½ cup fresh lemon juice
½ cup fresh lime juice
2 cups fresh orange juice
1 cup extra-virgin olive oil
2 jalapeño peppers, thinly sliced
4 garlic cloves, grated
2 thumb-size pieces fresh ginger, peeled and grated
Salt and pepper

Two 14-ounce packages extra-firm tofu, drained, pressed (see Efficiency Tip, page 49), and cut into bite-size cubes
¼ cup vegan mayo
Toothpicks
Lemon and/or lime slices, for garnish (optional)

To make the Citrus Marinade, in a large bowl, whisk together the marmalade, lemon juice, lime juice, orange juice, oil, jalapeño peppers, garlic, and ginger. Season with a healthy pinch of salt and pepper.

Transfer the marinade to one or two large casseroles or zip-top bags. Add the tofu cubes and submerge them in the marinade. Put the casseroles or bags in the fridge to let the tofu marinate for at least 1 hour.

Preheat the oven to 450°F. Line a baking sheet with parchment paper or a Silpat baking mat. Remove the tofu from the marinade, allowing the excess marinade to fall back into the bag. Be sure to reserve all the marinade, as you'll need it for the other recipes in this menu. Spread out the tofu in a single layer on the baking sheet, being careful not to crowd the pieces. There should be space between the cubes so they can brown evenly (if they don't all fit on one baking sheet, use a second baking sheet). Bake the tofu for 20 minutes, or until sufficiently browned on the top, then toss and bake for 20 more minutes, or until browned.

While the tofu bakes, in a small bowl whisk together 3 tablespoons of the Citrus Marinade and the vegan mayo. Remove the tofu from the oven and let cool. Serve at room temperature with toothpicks, the lemon and/or lime slices (if using), and the marinade-mayo mixture, a.k.a. "titrus dip," for dipping. If you like, fish out a few jalapeño slices from the marinade and place them artfully on the tofu and dip as a garnish.

Citrus Soba

8 ounces dried soba noodles (see WTF below)

½ cup Citrus Marinade (see Tofu-Citrus "Titrus" Dippers recipe, page 51)

2 tablespoons sesame oil

2 tablespoons low-sodium tamari

3 scallions, thinly sliced

Salt and pepper

Black and white sesame seeds, for garnish

Bring a large pot of water to a boil, and add a healthy pinch of salt. Drop in the noodles and cook, stirring often, for 5 to 6 minutes, or until tender. Drain the noodles and rinse thoroughly under cold running water, not only to stop the cooking but to rinse away excess starch, which would leave an unpleasant taste. Then drain again.

In a large bowl, whisk together the Citrus Marinade, sesame oil, and tamari. Add the noodles and scallions, and toss. Season with salt and pepper to taste, and garnish with sesame seeds.

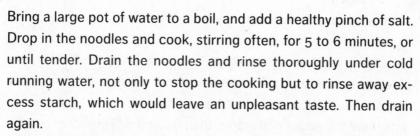

WTF are soba noodles? They are thin Japanese noodles made of buckwheat flour that can be served cold in a salad or hot in a broth. Since they cook quickly, they're perfect for happy hour. Find them in the Asian section of the grocery store, at the Asian market, or on the Interwebs.

Grilled Pineapple Salad

Four ½-inch-thick rounds fresh pineapple, with core

1 tablespoon extra-virgin olive oil

Salt and pepper

⅓ English or hothouse cucumber (about 5 ounces), thinly sliced

1 avocado, cubed

¼ cup thinly sliced red onion

3 tablespoons Citrus Marinade (see Tofu-Citrus "Titrus" Dippers recipe, page 51)

½ teaspoon finely chopped fresh mint

Heat the grill or a grill pan to high–very high. Brush each side of the pineapple slices with oil, and season with a little salt and pepper. Place the pineapple slices on the grill. Cook for 3 to 4 minutes, or until there are ample grill marks, then flip and grill the other side for 3 to 4 more minutes. Remove the pineapple from the grill and let cool. Cut the fruit away from the core and cut into bite-size pieces.

In a medium bowl, toss together the grilled pineapple, cucumber, avocado, red onion, Citrus Marinade, and mint. Season with salt and pepper to taste.

Nothing Rhymes with Citrus

SHOPPING LIST

PRODUCE

- Pineapple (1)
- Lemons (2)
- Limes (4)

  If you want to garnish the tofu with citrus slices, buy an extra lemon and/or lime.
- Avocado (1)
- English or hothouse cucumber (1)
- Jalapeño peppers (2)
- Scallions (1 bunch)
- Red onion (1 small)
- Garlic (4 cloves)
- Ginger (2 thumb-size pieces)
- Mint (1 bunch)

PANTRY

- Orange marmalade (½ cup)
- Dried soba noodles (8 ounces)
- Extra-virgin olive oil (8 fluid ounces [1 cup] plus 1 tablespoon)
- Sesame oil (2 tablespoons)
- Tamari, low-sodium (2 tablespoons)
- Sesame seeds, black and white (for garnish)
- Salt
- Pepper

MISCELLANEOUS

- Fresh orange juice (2 cups)
- Vegan mayo (¼ cup)
- Tofu, extra-firm (two 14-ounce packages)

6

NEW NEW ENGLAND

I didn't put any jackfruit dishes in the first book because, at the time, I found jackfruit (see WTF, page 58) difficult to come by. But over the past year, I've gotten emails from people in different parts of the country about how they saw my BBQ Jackfruit video and made the recipe at home. Evidently, it can be obtained more easily than I thought. I've since found websites that you can order it from.

Scan to watch the video.

So now I'm confident that putting a jackfruit recipe in this book will not be a waste of time. And this jackfruit recipe is probably the best one I've come up with to date. The carrot "fries" and seasoned oyster crackers are nothing to sneeze at, either...unless you take a big whiff of them; then you might sneeze because of all the spices.

LIBATION RECOMMENDATION

Get drunk on amber lagers and practice your New England accent. Say it with me: "They're in tha yahd, naht too faah, from tha caah." Bonus points if you can name the movie that line is from.

EFFICIENCY TIP

You can make the jackfruit mixture ahead of time and store it in the fridge for a day or two.

WTF is jackfruit? Grown in India, Southeast Asia, and the Caribbean, it is sweet and fruity when ripe. But when cooked from the young green state, it takes on the consistency of pulled pork or shredded crabmeat. It is very important that you use the "young" or "green" jackfruit that's packed in water or brine for this recipe, and not the ripe jackfruit, which is usually packed in syrup. It can be found in Indian or Asian markets, or on the Interwebs.

When the oven is up to temp, bake the oyster crackers first, so they have time to cool, then bake the carrot "fries" just before serving.

“Crab” Roll

2 tablespoons extra-virgin olive oil

Four 20-ounce cans young green jackfruit in water or brine, drained, rinsed, and roughly chopped (see WTF on page 58)

2 cups water

Two 5-inch pieces wakame (see WTF below)

½ cup finely diced celery

2 scallions, thinly sliced

¼ cup finely diced jicama

¾ cup vegan mayo

½ teaspoon seaweed powder (see WTF, next page)

2 teaspoons fresh lemon juice

2 tablespoons finely chopped fresh Italian parsley

Salt and pepper

8 small dinner rolls, split and toasted, if you like

In a large skillet, heat the oil over medium-high heat, and add the jackfruit. Don’t add any salt, since the wakame will add a salty note during the next step. Fry for 4 to 5 minutes, or until the jackfruit begins to brown, then toss and fry for 5 more minutes. Add the water and wakame, and bring to a boil. Reduce the heat to medium and simmer for 7 to 8 minutes, or until the liquid is absorbed. Remove the wakame and discard. Raise the heat to medium-high, and fry the jackfruit, stirring occasionally, for 8 to 10 minutes, or until the outsides and the stringy edges are crisp. Remove from the heat, and transfer to a large bowl to cool.

When the jackfruit is cool, add the celery, scallions, jicama, mayo, seaweed

WTF is wakame?

In addition to being a really fun word to say, wakame (pronounced WAH-kuh-may) is an edible seaweed that lends a subtly-sweet-yet-salty-from-the-sea flavor to soups, sauces, and broths. Find it in a Japanese market, in the Asian section of your grocery store, or on the Interwebs.

> **WTF** is seaweed powder? It's dried, ground-up seaweed that's a great source of vitamin B_{12}, calcium, minerals, iron, and iodine, and it makes things taste of the sea. Find it at health food stores or in the Asian section of your supermarket.

powder, lemon juice, and parsley, and mix until combined. Season with salt and pepper to taste. Place a heaping spoonful of the jackfruit mixture on each of the rolls to make little sandwiches.

Seasoned Oyster Crackers

4 cups oyster crackers

2 teaspoons extra-virgin olive oil

½ teaspoon smoked paprika

¼ teaspoon mustard powder

¼ teaspoon garlic powder

¼ teaspoon celery seeds

Preheat the oven to 400°F. Line a baking sheet with parchment paper or a Silpat baking mat.

In a large bowl, combine all the ingredients and toss until the crackers are well coated. Spread out the crackers in a single layer on the baking sheet. Bake for 6 to 8 minutes, or until slightly browned. Remove from the oven and let cool.

Old Bay Carrot "Fries"

1 pound carrots, cut into french fry–size pieces

1 tablespoon extra-virgin olive oil

1 tablespoon Old Bay seasoning

1 cup ketchup

2 tablespoons prepared horseradish

1 tablespoon finely chopped fresh Italian parsley

Preheat the oven to 400°F. Line 2 baking sheets with parchment paper or Silpat baking mats.

In a large bowl, toss the carrots with the oil and Old Bay seasoning. Spread out the carrots in a single layer on the baking sheets. Roast for 12 to 15 minutes, or until fork-tender and the edges are brown.

In a small bowl, whisk together the ketchup and horseradish. Sprinkle the "fries" with parsley. Serve with the ketchup for dipping.

New New England

SHOPPING LIST

PRODUCE

Lemon (1)
Jicama (1)
Celery (2 stalks)
Carrots (1 pound)
Scallions (1 bunch)
Italian parsley (1 bunch)

PANTRY

Extra-virgin olive oil (about ¼ cup)
Ketchup (1 cup)
Prepared horseradish (2 tablespoons)
Celery seeds (¼ teaspoon)
Garlic powder (¼ teaspoon)
Mustard powder (¼ teaspoon)
Old Bay seasoning (1 tablespoon)
Smoked paprika (½ teaspoon)
Salt
Pepper

ASIAN AISLE/MARKET

Jackfruit, young green, in water or brine (four 20-ounce cans)
Seaweed powder (½ teaspoon)
Wakame seaweed (two 5-inch pieces)

MISCELLANEOUS

Vegan mayo (¾ cup)
Small dinner rolls (8)
Oyster crackers (4 cups)

7 Papadilla, Don't Preach

Braised Scallion Papadillas

Fresh Corn and Jalapeño Salad

Nectarines with Mole-ish Stuff on Them

Shopping List

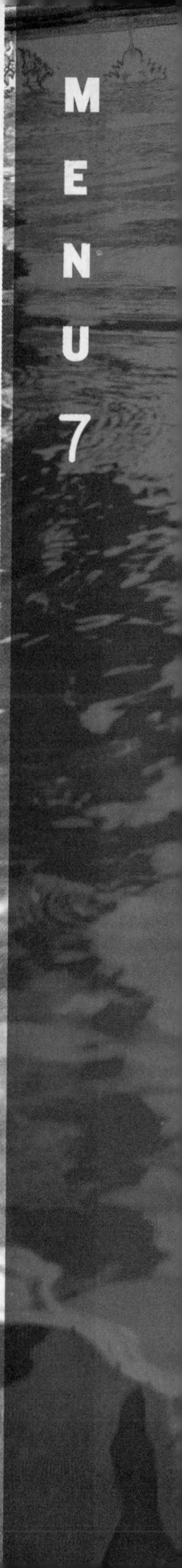

Papadilla. It's a word I made up for a quesadilla that's cooked with potatoes instead of cheese. I replaced *queso* with *papa*, and boom, I became a clever guy. That is, until I Googled my new word and saw that not only was it not a new word but its English translation is "fleshy part under the chin" or "double chin." I don't care. I'm sticking with it...but don't eat too many papadillas, or you might end up with a papadilla. The jokes won't all be this lame, I promise.

LIBATION RECOMMENDATION

Go with the Pomarita (see recipe, page 203) for this menu, or have a good Mexican beer.

EFFICIENCY TIP

Save time by roasting the jalapeño peppers and braising the scallions the day before or the morning you plan to serve this menu. Not only will you get those cooking processes out of the way, but you also won't have to wait for the peppers and scallions to cool before using them.

Braised Scallion Papadillas

3 tablespoons vegan margarine, plus more for the casserole

12 scallions, trimmed

½ cup water

1 pound russet potatoes, peeled and quartered

2 jalapeño peppers

½ cup unsweetened nondairy milk

2 teaspoons nutritional yeast

Salt and pepper

2 teaspoons extra-virgin olive oil

2 burrito-size (12-inch) flour tortillas, warmed

1 large beefsteak tomato, cut into 12 thin slices

Preheat the oven to 350°F. Lube up a large casserole with vegan margarine, and spread out the scallions in a single layer in the casserole. If you need to use two casseroles, so be it. Drop 1 tablespoon of the margarine on top of the scallions, breaking it up with your fingers to spread it around a bit. Add the water, cover with foil, and braise in the oven for 30 minutes.

Meanwhile, in a medium pot, cover the potatoes with cold water, and bring to a boil. Boil for 8 to 10 minutes, or until the chunks easily fall apart when you put a fork through them.

Once you get the scallions and potatoes started, you can roast the jalapeños. Place them directly on the burner of your gas stove or under a broiler. Roast them on one side for about 3 minutes, or until blackened and blistered, then turn and roast for about 3 more minutes, or until blackened and blistered on all sides. Place the roasted jalapeños in a paper bag with the top closed or in a bowl covered with plastic wrap. Let the jalapeños steam for at least 10 minutes, which further cooks them and makes the skin easier to remove.

By now the potatoes should be finished. Dump them into a colander to drain the water, and return them to the empty pot. Cook them over low heat for 1 to 2 minutes, to help dry them out. Pass the warm potatoes through a potato ricer or food mill into a bowl, or if you have not heeded the anti-mashing advice from my first book, mash them...like a caveman/cavewoman. Add the nondairy milk, the remaining 2 tablespoons margarine, and the nutritional yeast and gently fold everything together until well combined. Season with salt and pepper to taste. Set aside.

When the jalapeños are cool enough to handle, remove the stems, skin, and seeds, and cut them into small dice. Divide in half and set aside. Half of them are for the papadillas and half of them are for the Fresh Corn and Jalapeño Salad (see recipe, page 69).

At this point about 30 minutes will have passed, so remove the foil from the scallions and return them to the oven to cook uncovered for 15 more minutes. Remove from the oven and let cool. Slice 6 scallions thinly and set aside for the Fresh Corn and Jalapeño Salad (see recipe, page 69). Cut the remaining scallions into ½-inch pieces.

In a large skillet or on a griddle, heat the oil over medium heat. To assemble the papadillas, lay out the tortillas on a clean surface. Since we'll be folding these tortillas in half, we will only place ingredients on the right half, leaving the left half empty. Place ingredients on each tortilla as follows: First, lay down 3 slices of the tomato, and hit them with salt and pepper. Second, spread the potato mixture evenly over the tomatoes. Third, evenly scatter the scallions atop the potato mixture. Fourth, top the scallions with the remaining tomato slices, and season them with salt and pepper. Fold over the tortilla, and place in the skillet or on the griddle. Fry for 4 to 5 minutes, or until golden brown, then flip and fry the other side for 4 to 5 minutes. Cut each papadilla into quarters and serve.

Fresh Corn and Jalapeño Salad

2 ears raw corn, kernels cut from the cob

½ cup diced red bell pepper

6 braised scallions, sliced, reserved from the Braised Scallion Papadillas (see recipe, page 66)

1 roasted jalapeño pepper, diced, reserved from the Braised Scallion Papadillas (see recipe, page 66)

1 tablespoon roughly chopped fresh cilantro

2 teaspoons fresh lime juice

1 tablespoon extra-virgin olive oil

Salt and pepper

In a large bowl, toss the corn with the bell pepper, scallions, jalapeño pepper, cilantro, lime juice, and oil.

Nectarines with Mole-ish Stuff on Them

4 ripe nectarines, pitted and sliced into wedges

¼ teaspoon maple syrup

¼ teaspoon ground cinnamon

Pinch of ground nutmeg

Pinch of chili powder

Dark chocolate bar, for garnish

In a large bowl, toss the nectarines with the maple syrup, cinnamon, nutmeg, and chili powder until well coated. Transfer to a serving plate. With a zester or grater, shave dark chocolate onto the nectarines to your heart's desire.

Papadilla, Don’t Preach

PRODUCE

Nectarines (4)
Lime (1)
Beefsteak tomato (1 large)
Jalapeño peppers (2)
Red bell pepper (1)
Russet potatoes (1 pound)
Corn (2 ears)
Scallions (1 bunch of 12)
Cilantro (1 bunch)

PANTRY

Nutritional yeast (2 teaspoons)
Maple syrup (¼ teaspoon)
Extra-virgin olive oil (1 tablespoon plus 2 teaspoons)
Chili powder (just a pinch)
Ground cinnamon (¼ teaspoon)
Ground nutmeg (just a pinch)
Salt
Pepper

MISCELLANEOUS

Nondairy milk, unsweetened (½ cup)
Vegan margarine (about 4 tablespoons)
Dark chocolate bar (for garnish)
Flour tortillas, burrito-size (12-inch) (2)

8

LITTLE INDIA

Samosa Pizzas with Tamarind Date Chutney and Mint Chutney

Roasted Chana

Stuffed Dates

Shopping List

MENU 8

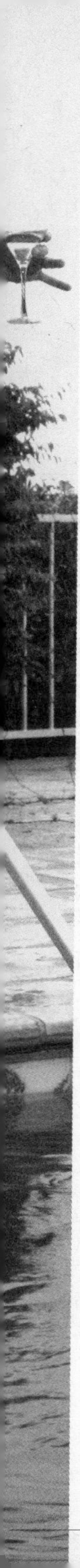

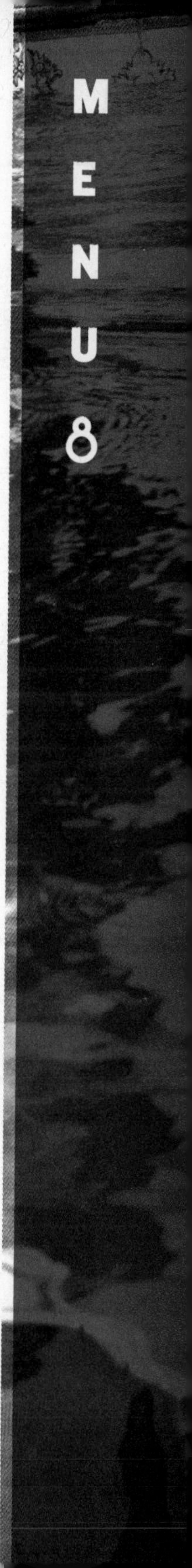

As you may have noticed on my Instagram feed, during the past year I have engaged in a love affair with Indian food. It's probably the only love affair that the Wife would not only tolerate but encourage. She (usually) benefits greatly from my experiments. However, she is not too thrilled when I try to do a choreographed Bollywood dance with her after dinner. She also doesn't like when I indulge in the affair behind her back. But it's really not my fault. I *have* to go to Samosa House to get spices for work, and if the best samosa in town is made three feet from where I buy my spices, what am I supposed to do? Not have a samosa or three?

I have to honor my love for samosas, but I want to save you the effort of making the pastry and doing any deep-frying, so I put the ingredients on a pizza.

LIBATION RECOMMENDATION

I made the Mangled Mango (see recipe, page 198) for this menu because its fruity nature is a great complement to the savory spices. The ginger beer ties it all together.

EFFICIENCY TIP

Get the roasted chana in the oven first, then proceed with the pizzas and dates. To save time, you can also stop by your nearest Indian market or eatery, and ask if you can buy the chutneys served with its samosas, so you don't have to make them from scratch.

Samosa Pizzas with Tamarind Date Chutney and Mint Chutney

1½ pounds russet potatoes, peeled and quartered
3 tablespoons extra-virgin olive oil
½ teaspoon ground coriander
Juice of ½ lime
2 scallions, thinly sliced
Pinch of Indian chili powder or ground cayenne pepper
Salt and black pepper
1 teaspoon minced peeled fresh ginger
¼ teaspoon cumin seeds
¼ teaspoon fennel seeds
½ teaspoon asafetida (hing; see WTF, page 76)
2 garlic cloves, minced
½ cup frozen peas, thawed
1 tablespoon finely chopped fresh cilantro, plus a few sprigs for garnish
Five 6-inch chapatis or whole-wheat tortillas
Tamarind Date Chutney (recipe follows)
Mint Chutney (recipe follows)

In a medium pot, cover the potatoes with cold water and bring to a boil. Boil for 5 to 7 minutes, or just until fork-tender. Drain and let cool. When the potatoes are cool enough to handle, cut into bite-size pieces, and transfer to a bowl. Toss the potatoes with 1 tablespoon of the olive oil, the coriander, lime juice, scallions, chili powder, and a healthy pinch of salt and black pepper.

In a large skillet, heat the remaining 2 tablespoons oil over medium heat. Add the ginger, cumin seeds, fennel seeds, and asafetida, and cook for 2 minutes. Add the garlic and cook, stirring often, for 2 more minutes. Add the potatoes and cook for 3 to 4 minutes, stirring occasionally. Add the peas and cilantro, and cook for

1 more minute, or until heated through. Transfer the potato mixture to a bowl and set aside.

Line a baking sheet with parchment paper or a Silpat baking mat. Lay the chapatis on the baking sheet. Spread the Tamarind Date Chutney on them as you would a pizza sauce, leaving a narrow perimeter of chapati unsauced, and top with the potato mixture. Bake for 5 to 7 minutes, or until the edges and bottom of the chapatis become crisp. Remove from the oven, and cut each pizza into 4 pieces. Garnish with cilantro sprigs. Serve with Mint Chutney on the side, so your guests can spoon as much or as little as they like onto the pizzas.

TAMARIND DATE CHUTNEY

WTF are these crazy things you speak of? Oh, you must be talking about asafetida and amchoor. Well, asafetida is a spice also known as hing, ting, and devil's dung (how pleasant). It has a rather pungent scent when raw, but once it's cooked it has a mild leek-like flavor. Amchoor is a powder made of dried green mangoes, and it has a sour, fruity flavor. You can find both ingredients at the Indian market or on the Interwebs. Once you have them, a little goes a long way, so you won't have to buy them very often.

4 medjool dates
1 cup water
1 teaspoon tamarind paste
1 teaspoon agave nectar
½ teaspoon garam masala
¼ teaspoon amchoor (see WTF at left)
¼ teaspoon turmeric
⅛ teaspoon Indian chili powder or cayenne pepper

If the dates have pits, remove and discard them. Roughly chop the dates. In a small saucepan, combine all the ingredients and bring to a simmer over medium heat. Simmer for 10 minutes, or until the dates are very soft. Transfer the mixture to a blender or food processor, and puree for 30 seconds, or until smooth.

MINT CHUTNEY

¾ cup water
1 thumb-size piece fresh ginger, peeled and sliced
¼ medium red onion, roughly chopped
1 small Indian or Thai green chile, roughly chopped
1 bunch fresh cilantro, roughly chopped
¼ packed cup fresh mint leaves
Juice of ½ lime

Place all ingredients in a blender or food processor, and puree for 30 seconds, or until smooth.

Roasted Chana

Two 15-ounce cans chickpeas, rinsed, drained, and patted dry

1 teaspoon tomato paste

1 tablespoon canola oil

½ teaspoon grated peeled fresh ginger

2 garlic cloves, grated

½ teaspoon onion powder

½ teaspoon ground cumin

½ teaspoon ground coriander

½ teaspoon garam masala

¼ teaspoon Indian chili powder or ground cayenne pepper

½ teaspoon salt

Preheat the oven to 375°F. Line a baking sheet with parchment paper or a Silpat baking mat. In a large bowl, combine all the ingredients and toss until the chickpeas are well coated with the spices. Spread out the chickpeas in a single layer on the baking sheet. Roast for 30 to 40 minutes, or until crisp. Let cool and serve at room temperature.

Stuffed Dates

12 medjool dates

1 English cucumber, peeled

12 whole roasted unsalted almonds

Smoked sea salt or regular sea salt (optional)

With a paring knife, make a lengthwise slit in each date, being sure not to cut all the way through. If the dates have pits, remove and discard them. With a vegetable peeler, shave a long flat ribbon from the cucumber. Rotate the cucumber and then shave another ribbon. Repeat shaving and rotating the cucumber until you have 12 ribbons, each about 3 to 4 inches in length. Wrap each ribbon around 1 almond. Stuff each cucumber-wrapped almond into a date. If desired, sprinkle the stuffed dates with smoked sea salt, if you have it, or regular sea salt. Serve.

Scan to watch the video.

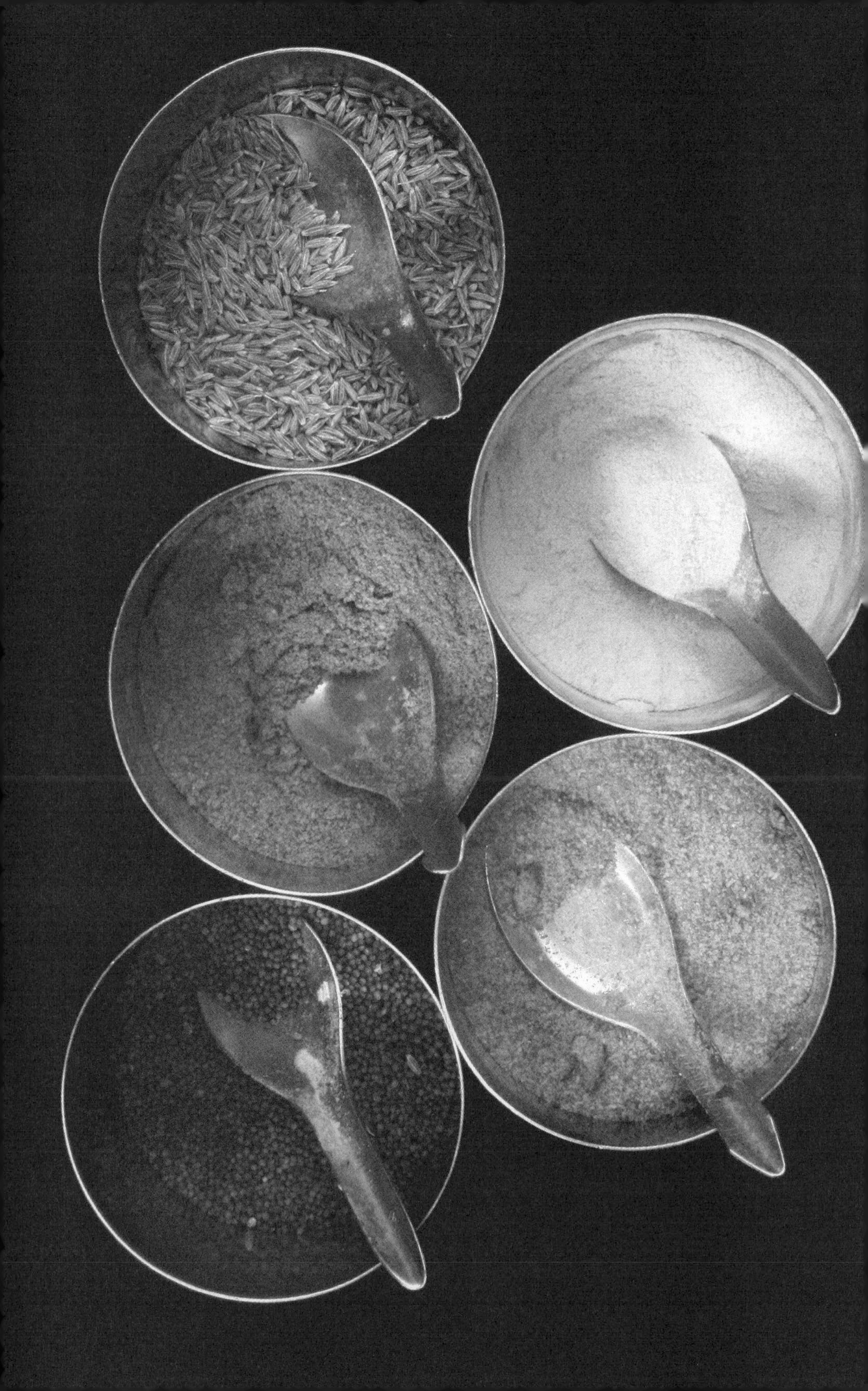

SHOPPING LIST

Little India

PRODUCE

- Medjool dates (16)
- Lime (1)
- Russet potatoes (1½ pounds)
- English cucumber (1)
- Scallions (1 bunch)
- Red onion (1 medium)
- Garlic (4 cloves)
- Ginger (2 thumb-size pieces)
- Cilantro (2 bunches)
- Mint (1 bunch)

PANTRY

- Chickpeas (two 15-ounce cans)
- Tomato paste (1 teaspoon)
- Agave nectar (1 teaspoon)
- Extra-virgin olive oil (3 tablespoons)
- Canola oil (1 tablespoon)
- Almonds, whole roasted unsalted (12)
- Ground coriander (1 teaspoon)
- Ground cumin (½ teaspoon)
- Cumin seeds (¼ teaspoon)
- Fennel seeds (¼ teaspoon)
- Garam masala (1 teaspoon)
- Onion powder (½ teaspoon)
- Turmeric (¼ teaspoon)
- Smoked sea salt (optional; for sprinkling)
- Salt
- Pepper

INDIAN MARKET

- Indian or Thai green chile (1 small)
- Asafetida (hing) (½ teaspoon)
- Amchoor (¼ teaspoon)
- Indian chili powder or cayenne pepper (½ teaspoon)
- Tamarind paste (1 teaspoon)
- Chapatis or whole-wheat tortillas (five 6-inch)

MISCELLANEOUS

- Frozen peas (one 16-ounce bag)

9
LITTLE BRITAIN

MENU 9

Allo, guvnah!! That's about as far as my British accent goes. Pretty sweet, though, huh? You should hear it in person. It didn't work too well that time I dressed up as Harry Potter for Halloween, but it was better than nothing. Anyway, I try to minimize utensil usage as much as I can at happy hour. And a handheld banger and mash roll is a perfect — and delicious — example of that effort.

LIBATION RECOMMENDATION

An English pale ale would be great with this menu. Just be sure to consult Barnivore.com to confirm that your beer is vegan.

EFFICIENCY TIP

You could make the gravy the day before, then reheat it before serving. You could also make the Mushy Pea Fritters up until they are ready to be fried, then spread them out on a plate covered with plastic wrap and refrigerate them overnight. Just be sure to allow them to return to room temperature before frying.

Banger and Mash Rolls with Quick Gravy

3 tablespoons vegan margarine
1 medium yellow onion, sliced
Salt and pepper
1 pound Yukon Gold potatoes, peeled and quartered
2 teaspoons whole-grain mustard
3 tablespoons unsweetened nondairy milk, at room temperature
12 green cabbage leaves (each about the size of your palm)
2 teaspoons extra-virgin olive oil
Four 3-ounce store-bought vegan sausages or 4 Pretend Italian Sausages (see recipe, page 29)
Quick Gravy (recipe follows), warmed

In a large skillet, melt 1 tablespoon of the margarine over medium-low heat. Add the onion and a pinch of salt and cook for 25 to 30 minutes, or until soft and caramelized. Transfer to a bowl and loosely cover with foil to keep warm.

In a medium pot, cover the potatoes with cold water and bring to a boil. Boil for 8 to 10 minutes, or until the chunks easily fall apart when you put a fork through them. Drain the potatoes and return them to the empty pot. Cook them over low heat for 1 or 2 minutes, to help dry them out. Pass the warm potatoes through a potato ricer or food mill into a bowl, or simply mash them. Add the cooked onions, the remaining 2 tablespoons margarine, the mustard, and the nondairy milk, and gently fold everything together until well combined. Season with salt and pepper to taste. Loosely cover with foil to keep warm.

Using a steamer basket, steam the cabbage leaves until soft and pliable, about 4 minutes. Uncover the pan, turn off the heat, and leave the cabbage leaves in the steamer until ready to use.

In a large skillet, heat the olive oil over medium-high heat. Add the sausages and cook until browned, about 2 minutes per side. Cut each link into thirds, place them in a bowl, and loosely cover with foil to keep warm.

To assemble, reheat the cabbage in the steamer basket over high heat for 2 minutes. You just want to warm it up a bit. Lay out the cabbage leaves on a clean work surface, and spread a thin layer of mashed potatoes on the leaves. Place 1 piece of sausage in the middle of each leaf, and roll up the leaves into cone shapes, so one end is closed and the other end is open. If the banger and mash rolls are cool, place them in a 300°F oven for a few minutes until warmed through. Place on a platter with the gravy on the side.

QUICK GRAVY

3 tablespoons vegan margarine
3 garlic cloves, minced
3 tablespoons unbleached all-purpose flour
1 teaspoon balsamic vinegar
1 tablespoon low-sodium tamari
3 cups vegetable stock, warmed
Salt and pepper

In a small pot, melt the margarine over medium heat. Add the garlic, cook for 2 minutes, stirring occasionally, then stir in the flour. Cook, stirring constantly, for 3 to 4 minutes, or until the flour-margarine mixture turns to a blond color. Add the vinegar and tamari, and cook for 2 more minutes. Add the vegetable stock, ½ cup at a time, and stir to prevent lumps from forming. Simmer for 5 more minutes, or until thick enough to coat the back of a spoon. Season with salt and pepper to taste. Keep warm over low heat.

Mushy Pea Fritters with Curry-Mint Dipping Sauce

Canola, peanut, or any other high-heat oil, for deep-frying

2 cups frozen peas, thawed and patted dry

1 teaspoon finely chopped fresh mint

1 tablespoon plus 1 teaspoon plain vegan yogurt

1 teaspoon fresh lemon juice

4 scallions, green parts only, thinly sliced

½ teaspoon salt

Pepper

2 teaspoons arrowroot

½ cup chickpea flour, plus more as needed

1 teaspoon baking powder

1½ teaspoons curry powder

The Sexy Sprinkle (see recipe, page 42) for dusting (optional)

Curry-Mint Dipping Sauce (recipe follows)

Preheat the oven to 200°F. Line a plate with paper towels and set it next to the stove. Pour oil to a depth of at least 3 inches in a medium pot, high-sided pan, or deep fryer. Heat the oil over medium-high heat until it registers 350°F on a deep-frying thermometer, or until a tiny sprinkle of flour froths when it hits the oil.

In a blender or food processor, process the peas, mint, yogurt, lemon juice, scallions, salt, and a couple grinds of pepper, scraping down the sides as needed, until combined and roughly chopped — you do not want a smooth puree. In a large bowl, combine the arrowroot, chickpea flour, baking powder, and curry powder. Add the pea mixture to the flour mixture, and fold them together until thoroughly combined. Take a bit of the pea-flour mixture in your hand and make a little ball; if it holds together and isn't sticking to your hands, it's ready. If it's sticky, mix in a touch more flour.

Portion out the fritters with a tablespoon. You should get about 24 fritters. Roll each fritter into a tight ball, then slightly flatten it.

Working in batches, gently drop the fritters into the oil, being careful not to crowd the pot. Fry the fritters for 3 to 4 minutes, turning them with tongs halfway through cooking to brown on both sides.

Using a slotted spoon, transfer the fritters to the paper towel–lined plate. Dust them immediately with a liberal amount of the Sexy Sprinkle (or just salt and pepper), if desired, and keep warm in the oven. Fry the remaining fritters in the same way, allowing the oil to return to 350°F before each batch. Serve warm or at room temperature with Curry-Mint Dipping Sauce.

CURRY-MINT DIPPING SAUCE

½ cup plain vegan yogurt

1½ teaspoons finely chopped fresh mint

1 teaspoon lemon juice

1 teaspoon curry powder

1 tablespoon water

Salt and pepper

In a blender or food processor, combine the yogurt, mint, lemon juice, curry powder, and water, and puree for 30 seconds, or until smooth. Season with salt and pepper to taste.

SHOPPING LIST

Little Britain

PRODUCE

Lemon (1)
Yukon Gold potatoes (1 pound)
Green cabbage (1 head)
Scallions (1 bunch)
Yellow onion (1 medium)
Garlic (3 cloves)
Mint (1 bunch)

PANTRY

Unbleached all-purpose flour (3 tablespoons)
Chickpea flour (about ¾ cup)
Baking powder (1 teaspoon)
Arrowroot (2 teaspoons)
Vegetable stock (24 fluid ounces [3 cups])
Extra-virgin olive oil (2 teaspoons)
Canola, peanut, or any other high-heat oil (1 or 2 quarts, depending on the size of your deep-frying vessel)
Balsamic vinegar (1 teaspoon)
Tamari, low-sodium (1 tablespoon)
Whole-grain mustard (2 teaspoons)
Curry powder (2½ teaspoons)
Salt
Pepper
Unrefined granulated sugar (1 teaspoon)
Nutritional yeast (½ teaspoon)
Granulated garlic or garlic powder (1 teaspoon)
Granulated onion or onion powder (1 teaspoon)
Smoked paprika (1 teaspoon)

You'll need these items if you're making the Sexy Sprinkle (see recipe, page 42), an optional ingredient in the Mushy Pea Fritters.

MISCELLANEOUS

Nondairy milk, unsweetened (3 tablespoons)
Vegan margarine (6 tablespoons)

Plain vegan yogurt (about ¾ cup)
Frozen peas (one 16-ounce bag)
Vegan sausages (four 3-ounce) — OR if you want to make my Pretend Italian Sausages, you'll need:

- Russet potatoes (½ pound)
- Yellow onion (1 small)
- Garlic (3 cloves)
- Chickpea flour or all-purpose flour (1 tablespoon)
- Vital wheat gluten (1 cup)
- Nutritional yeast (1 tablespoon)
- White beans (one 15-ounce can)
- Sun-dried tomatoes, chopped oil-packed (1 tablespoon)
- Tamari, low-sodium (¼ cup)
- Vegetable bouillon powder (½ teaspoon)
- Celery seeds (¼ teaspoon)
- Chile flakes (¼ teaspoon)
- Fennel seeds (½ teaspoon)
- Garlic powder (½ teaspoon)
- Onion powder (½ teaspoon)
- Ground sage (just a pinch)
- Dried thyme (just a pinch)

10

REALLY LITTLE ITALY

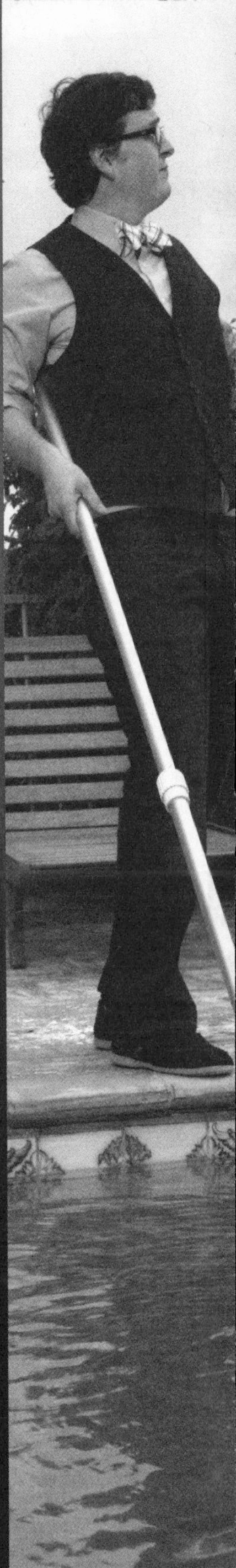

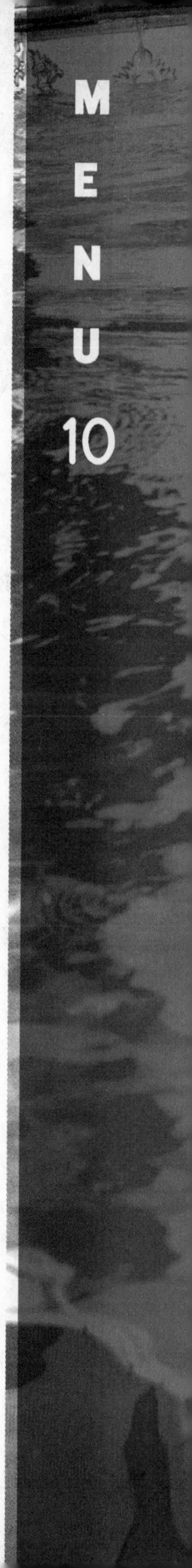

MENU 10

You know how sometimes there's a break in the clouds, and brilliant yet fleeting rays of light come shining through? That's what happened here. The cloud that usually encircles my brain opened up for a brief moment while I was looking in my cabinet for a pack of seaweed snacks that I knew was hiding in the back. I spotted a box of rigatoni, and out of nowhere I thought, "rigatoni poppers." I briefly pondered what to stuff into them, quickly realizing that the cashew ricotta from my first book was the obvious choice.

I never found those seaweed snacks, but I still go searching for them, in an attempt to recreate this moment of inspiration.

LIBATION RECOMMENDATION

The Figgy Lifting Drink (see recipe, page 194) is a great complement to this menu, as its bubbly properties help lighten the rich poppers, and the figs tie into the asparagus and fig dish. You could also grab a bottle of prosecco to enjoy here.

EFFICIENCY TIP

Unfortunately, breading the rigatoni poppers ahead of time and refrigerating would yield a gummy coating, so you have to do those just before frying. However, you can cut and skewer the watermelon, and make the basil-mint rub in the morning or the day before. Then just brush on the rub before grilling.

Rigatoni Poppers

Scan to watch the video.

4 ounces rigatoni (about 40 pieces)

1 cup unbleached all-purpose flour

Salt and pepper

2 cups Cashew Ricotta (recipe follows)

½ cup water

½ cup arrowroot

½ cup seasoned bread crumbs

Canola, vegetable, or any other high-heat oil, for deep-frying

Roughly chopped fresh Italian parsley, for garnish

1½ cups marinara sauce, warmed

Bring a large pot of salted water to a boil, and drop in your rigatoni. Cook, stirring often, for just 7 minutes. The rigatoni will be very al dente, but that's okay since we'll be cooking them again. Drain and let dry in a colander for a couple of minutes. Spread out the flour on a large plate, making sure that it's at least ⅛ inch deep. Season with a bit of salt and pepper. Place the rigatoni pieces on the flour so that they are standing on one end, with one opening in the flour and one opening facing up. Using a piping bag, fill each rigatoni piece with Cashew Ricotta.

Once the rigatoni are stuffed, set up your breading station. In a bowl, whisk together the water and arrowroot. Spread out the bread crumbs on a large plate. Line a baking sheet with wax paper so that you have somewhere to place the breaded rigatoni. To bread the rigatoni, working in batches, roll the stuffed rigatoni in the flour, making sure to coat the open ends, then dunk them in the arrowroot slurry, coat them in the bread crumbs, and place them on the baking sheet.

Preheat the oven to 200°F. Line a plate with paper towels and set it next to the stove. Pour oil to a depth of at least 2 inches into a pot, high-sided pan, or deep fryer, and heat over medium-high heat until it registers 350°F on a deep-frying thermometer, or until a tiny sprinkle of flour froths when it hits the oil. Working in batches, fry the rigatoni pieces for 3 to 4 minutes, turning them with tongs every minute or so to ensure that they brown on all sides.

Using a slotted spoon, transfer the rigatoni poppers to the paper towel–lined plate. Season immediately with salt and pepper and keep warm in the oven. Fry the remaining rigatoni poppers in the same way, allowing the oil to return to 350°F before each batch.

Pile the rigatoni poppers on a large plate, garnish with parsley, and serve with the marinara for dipping.

CASHEW RICOTTA

2 cups whole raw cashews
One 14-ounce can artichoke hearts, drained, rinsed, and roughly chopped
2 tablespoons fresh lemon juice
1 cup water
1½ teaspoons salt, plus more as needed
1 garlic clove
1 heaping tablespoon nutritional yeast
2 teaspoons extra-virgin olive oil
Pepper

In a medium pot, cover the cashews with water, and boil for 8 minutes to soften them up. (If you've got a high-powered blender like a Vitamix or Blendtec, you don't need to soften the cashews.) Drain and let cool. In a food processor or blender, process the cashews until they're finely ground. Add the artichokes, lemon juice, water, 1½ teaspoons salt, garlic, nutritional yeast, and oil, and puree until mostly smooth but still somewhat grainy. Season with more salt and pepper to taste.

You'll end up with about 3 cups of cashew ricotta. If you don't use it all right away, store the excess in an airtight container in the fridge for up to 4 days or in the freezer for up to 1 month.

Grilled Asparagus and Figs

¾ pound asparagus, trimmed

4 large Black Mission figs, halved lengthwise

1 tablespoon extra-virgin olive oil

Salt and pepper

Splash of balsamic vinegar

3 fresh basil leaves, cut into chiffonade (see WTF below)

Heat the grill or a grill pan to medium-high. In a large bowl, toss the asparagus and figs with the oil, and salt and pepper to taste. Place the asparagus and figs, cut side down, on the grill, making sure they sizzle. If they don't sizzle, keep 'em off dat grizzle. (I know, we should be done with the -izzles by now, huh? I'm still hanging on.) Grill the asparagus for 3 to 4 minutes, then flip and grill the other side for 3 to 4 minutes. Grill the figs for 4 or 5 minutes, or until tender with ample grill markage. Remove the figs and asparagus from the grill and let cool. When they are cool enough to handle, cut the asparagus spears into 1-inch pieces on the bias and thinly slice the figs lengthwise. Toss the asparagus and figs with the balsamic vinegar and basil. Season with salt and pepper to taste.

WTF is a chiffonade? I know it sounds super French and froufrou, but it's quite easy. Stack several leaves of whatever you are chiffonading on top of each other. Then roll them up tight like you would roll a cigar. Heh, what a silly thing to say — I mean, who has ever actually rolled a cigar? I imagine, however, you have probably rolled something at some point in your life, so just go with the method of rolling you're used to. Once you have rolled the leaves, thinly slice them crosswise to produce fancy little ribbons.

Grilled Basil-Mint Watermelon Skewers

8 wooden skewers

1 tablespoon roughly chopped fresh tarragon

¼ packed cup fresh basil leaves

¼ packed cup fresh mint leaves

¼ cup chopped toasted pecans

2 teaspoons fresh lemon juice

¼ cup extra-virgin olive oil

2 teaspoons agave nectar

1 tablespoon water

Salt and pepper

One 2-pound seedless watermelon, rind removed, cut into 1-inch cubes

Soak the skewers in water for at least 30 minutes so they don't burn on the grill. Heat the grill or a grill pan to very high.

In a food processor, combine the tarragon, basil, mint, pecans, lemon juice, oil, agave nectar, and water, and puree until smooth. Season with salt and pepper to taste.

Place 4 or 5 cubes of watermelon on each skewer, and brush with a generous amount of the herb mixture. Place the skewers on the grill diagonally, so that as much of the surface of the watermelon touches the grill as possible, and DO NOT TOUCH THEM for 3 minutes. Then check to see that the watermelon has grill marks. Once it does, flip the skewers over and grill the other side for 3 minutes.

Really Little Italy

PRODUCE

Seedless watermelon (one 2-pound)
Black Mission figs (4 large)
Lemon (1)
Asparagus (¾ pound)
Garlic (1 clove)
Basil (1 bunch)
Italian parsley (1 bunch)
Mint (1 bunch)
Tarragon (1 bunch)

PANTRY

Unbleached all-purpose flour (1 cup)
Arrowroot (½ cup)
Nutritional yeast (1 heaping tablespoon)
Seasoned bread crumbs (½ cup)
Marinara sauce (12 fluid ounces [1½ cups])
Artichoke hearts (one 14-ounce can)
Agave nectar (2 teaspoons)
Rigatoni (4 ounces)
Canola, vegetable, or any other high-heat oil (1 or 2 quarts, depending on the size of your deep-frying vessel)
Extra-virgin olive oil (about 6 tablespoons)
Balsamic vinegar (just a splash)
Cashews, whole raw (2 cups)
Pecans, chopped toasted (about ⅓ cup)
Salt
Pepper

MISCELLANEOUS

Wooden skewers (8)

11 THE FIXINS BAR

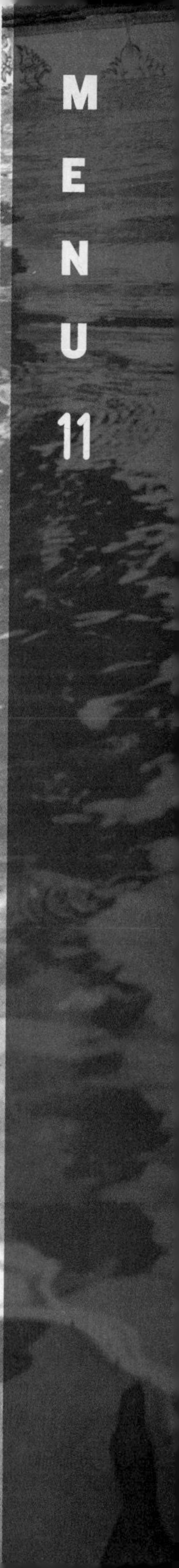

Keeping with my anti-utensil motif, I've taken something that once required a fork and even possibly a knife to eat — a baked potato — and, basically, put it on a pizza, making it a handheld wonder of creamy, crispy, savory, um, wonderment. There's nothing about this that is not awesome.

LIBATION RECOMMENDATION

A dark lager is the way to go here.

EFFICIENCY TIP

Take care of making the potatoes and putting the flatbread together and in the oven first. Then you'll have a nice pocket of time during which to handle the toppings.

Loaded Baked Potato Flatbread

1½ pounds Yukon Gold potatoes, peeled and quartered

2 tablespoons thinly sliced fresh chives

¼ cup vegan margarine

⅔ cup unsweetened soy creamer or nondairy milk, warmed or at room temperature

Salt and pepper

Extra-virgin olive oil for the baking sheet and brushing the dough

1 pound store-bought pizza dough or Basic Pizza Dough (see recipe, page 13), at room temperature

12 ounces vegan cheddar cheeze, shredded

Toppings

2 scallions, thinly sliced

8 ounces store-bought vegan bacon or 16 strips Tempeh Bacon (recipe follows), browned and finely chopped

3 Roma tomatoes, seeded and diced

One 15-ounce can vegan chili, warmed

1½ cups vegan sour cream

Preheat the oven to 400°F. In a medium pot, cover the potatoes with cold water and bring to a boil. Boil for 8 to 10 minutes, or until the chunks easily fall apart when you put a fork through them. Drain the potatoes and return them to the empty pot. Cook them over low heat for 1 to 2 minutes to help dry them out. Pass the warm potatoes through a potato ricer or food mill into a bowl, or simply mash them. Add the chives, margarine, and creamer and gently fold everything together until combined. Season with salt and pepper to taste. Loosely cover with foil to keep warm.

Grease up a 9½-by-13-inch baking sheet with oil. On a floured surface, roll the pizza dough into a large rectangle that is approximately 16 inches long and 13 inches wide. Transfer the dough to the baking sheet. Brush the top of the dough with oil and spread the mashed potatoes as you would a pizza sauce, leaving a narrow perimeter of dough uncovered. Top with the cheddar. Bake for 15 to 17 minutes, or until the edges and bottom are browned and the cheddar is melted. Remove from the oven, and cut the flatbread into 12 squares. Serve with the toppings on the side.

TEMPEH BACON

Scan to watch the video.

½ cup low-sodium tamari
1½ tablespoons apple cider vinegar
1 teaspoon garlic powder
1 teaspoon paprika
2 teaspoons molasses
2 teaspoons vegan Worcestershire sauce
1 drop liquid smoke
Pepper
One 8-ounce package tempeh, sliced into ⅛-inch-thick strips
Extra-virgin olive oil for frying (optional)

In a medium bowl, whisk together the tamari, vinegar, garlic powder, paprika, molasses, Worcestershire, liquid smoke, and a couple grinds of pepper. Pour the marinade into a zip-top bag, add the tempeh slices, and gently slosh them around so they get coated. Squeeze the bag to suck out as much air as possible, and zip it closed. Put the bag in the fridge to let the tempeh marinate for at least 8 hours (24 hours is ideal).

To cook the bacon, remove the tempeh from the marinade, letting the excess marinade fall away from the strips, and either bake at 375°F for about 10 minutes or fry in a pan with a little oil over medium heat for about 3 minutes per side, until browned.

If you don't use all the strips right away, store the remaining ones in an airtight container in the fridge for up to 3 days or in the freezer for up to 1 month.

The Fixins Bar

PRODUCE

Roma tomatoes (3)
Yukon Gold potatoes (1½ pounds)
Scallions (1 bunch)
Chives (1 bunch)

PANTRY

Vegan chili (one 15-ounce can)
Extra-virgin olive oil (for brushing)
Salt
Pepper

MISCELLANEOUS

Soy creamer or nondairy milk, unsweetened (⅔ cup)
Vegan cheddar cheeze (12 ounces)
Vegan margarine (¼ cup)
Vegan sour cream (1½ cups)
Vegan bacon (8 ounces) — OR if you want to make my Tempeh Bacon, you'll need:
- Molasses (2 teaspoons)
- Extra-virgin olive oil (for frying; optional)
- Apple cider vinegar (1½ tablespoons)
- Vegan Worcestershire sauce (2 teaspoons)
- Tamari, low-sodium (½ cup)
- Liquid smoke (1 drop)
- Garlic powder (1 teaspoon)
- Paprika (1 teaspoon)
- Tempeh (one 8-ounce package)

Pizza dough (1 pound) — OR if you want to make my Basic Pizza Dough, you'll need:
- Unbleached all-purpose flour (3 cups, plus more for dusting the work surface)
- Active dry yeast (one 7-gram package or 2¼ teaspoons)
- Agave nectar (1 tablespoon)
- Extra-virgin olive oil (about 2 tablespoons)

12

CHARRED AND ROASTED

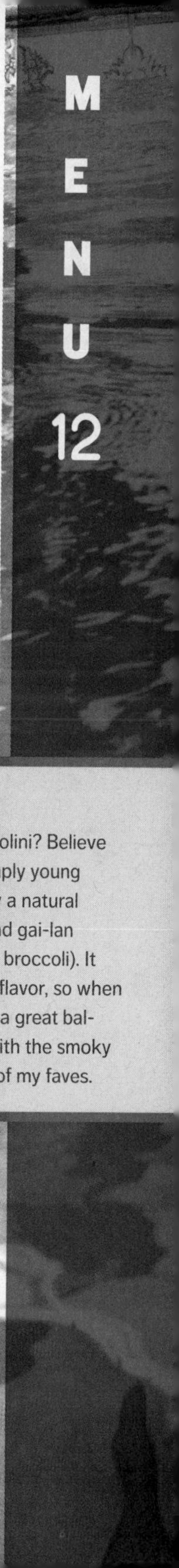

MENU 12

I can't get enough broccolini. When prepared properly (as I'm about to show you), there's nothing better than those al dente stalks, with crispy, slightly blackened florets on the ends. Broccolini is great either by itself; tossed with pasta, garlic, and olive oil; or on a pizza. For this happy hour, I serve broccolini alongside roasted peppers stuffed with hummus and arugula, and crackers with sunflower seed spread.

LIBATION RECOMMENDATION

I really like the Burn Relief (see recipe, page 199) or the Figgy Lifting Drink (see recipe, page 194) for this menu, as they nicely balance the charred, smoky flavors.

WTF is broccolini? Believe it or not, it is not simply young broccoli. It's actually a natural hybrid of broccoli and gai-lan (also called Chinese broccoli). It has a slightly sweet flavor, so when you grill it, you have a great balance of the sweet with the smoky and savory. It's one of my faves.

EFFICIENCY TIP

This menu is pretty fast no matter what, but using a store-bought hummus for the Roasted Pepper Rolls makes things even faster. Blanch the broccolini first, then tackle the rest of the menu while it dries. Once the rolls and Sunflower Seed Spread are ready to go, finish the broccolini and serve.

Charred Broccolini

14 ounces broccolini (see WTF, page 109) or baby broccoli

2 teaspoons extra-virgin olive oil

1 garlic clove, grated

Pinch of chile flakes

Salt and pepper

½ lemon

Bring a large pot of salted water to a boil. Have an ice bath standing by. Drop the broccolini into the boiling water and blanch for 90 seconds. When you can insert a fork somewhat easily, but not too easily, into the thickest part of the stalk, remove the broccolini from the water and submerge in the ice bath immediately. Once the broccolini are cool, you have to get them very dry, so let them drain in a colander, spin them in a salad spinner, dab them with paper towels, or even drive around the block a few times holding them out the window…just get them superdry.

Heat the grill or a grill pan to very high. In a large bowl, toss the broccolini with the olive oil, garlic, chile flakes, and salt and pepper to taste. Place the broccolini on the hot grill. Grill for 2 to 3 minutes per side, or until the florets get charred and some grill markage occurs on the stalks. Transfer to a serving plate, and squeeze the juice from the lemon over the broccolini just before serving.

Roasted Pepper Rolls

One 10-ounce jar roasted red bell peppers, patted dry and cut into 1½-inch-wide strips (12 strips)
½ cup hummus
½ packed cup baby arugula
12 pitted kalamata olives
12 toothpicks
Extra-virgin olive oil, for garnish
Balsamic vinegar, for garnish
Salt and pepper
4 fresh basil leaves, cut into chiffonade (see WTF, page 97)

Slather the inside of each roasted pepper strip with a thin layer of hummus and top with a few arugula leaves. Tightly roll the roasted pepper strips away from you, making sure that the seam is on top when rolling is complete. Place 1 olive on top of each seam, and put a toothpick through the olive and all the way through the roasted pepper roll. Arrange the rolls artfully on some sort of fancy tray or plate, and drizzle with oil and vinegar. Season with salt and pepper to taste, and garnish with basil.

Sunflower Seed Spread with Crackers

1 cup hulled roasted salted sunflower seeds, plus more for garnish
2 tablespoons extra-virgin olive oil, plus more for garnish
¼ cup water
2 teaspoons fresh lemon juice
2 teaspoons nutritional yeast
1½ teaspoons red wine vinegar
Salt and pepper
Pinch of smoked paprika
Assorted crackers

In a food processor or blender, process the sunflower seeds until finely ground. Add 2 tablespoons oil, the water, the lemon juice, the nutritional yeast, the vinegar, a pinch of salt, and a pinch of pepper. Process for 1 to 2 minutes, occasionally scraping down the sides of the bowl, until smooth. Season with salt and pepper to taste. Put the spread in a small serving bowl, and garnish with a splash of oil, a few sunflower seeds, and the paprika. Serve with crackers.

Charred and Roasted

PRODUCE

- Lemons (2)
- Baby arugula (½ packed cup)
- Broccolini or baby broccoli (14 ounces)
- Garlic (1 clove)
- Basil (1 bunch)

PANTRY

- Nutritional yeast (2 teaspoons)
- Roasted red peppers (one 10-ounce jar)
- Extra-virgin olive oil (about ¼ cup)
- Balsamic vinegar (for garnish)
- Red wine vinegar (1½ teaspoons)
- Kalamata olives, pitted (12)
- Sunflower seeds, roasted salted (1 cup, plus more for garnish)
- Chile flakes (just a pinch)
- Smoked paprika (just a pinch)
- Salt
- Pepper

MISCELLANEOUS

- Hummus (½ cup)
- Assorted crackers
- Toothpicks (12)

13

THE HAPPIEST MEAL: LITTLE MACS AND (REAL) SWEET POTATO FRIES

Little Macs with Very, Very Special Sauce

Baked Sweet Potato "Fries" with Adobo Dipping Sauce

Shopping List

For this menu I'm using actual sweet potatoes for the "fries" (which are actually baked). Everyone else knows "sweet potato fries" to be orange and sweet...but those aren't sweet potatoes — they're yams! (See WTF at right.) So why am I using sweet potatoes instead? The same reason I started wearing a bow tie: to be different and to get attention. And they taste pretty darn good too — slightly sweet with smoky spices and a great creamy texture on the inside. They're a hell of a lot more interesting than the regular old french fries that would accompany the, ahem, larger version of this burger. I think after all is said and done, these "fries" will be "America's favorite." I hope so, for America's sake. If you're so inclined, give each of your guests a little crappy toy that they can throw away as soon as they get home.

WTF is the difference between sweet potatoes and yams? There are so many botanical differences that my head almost exploded when I was reading and trying to understand them. For me to even attempt to regurgitate what I probably didn't even learn would be useless. Basically, sweet potatoes have a light-colored skin and flesh and are just slightly sweet. Yams, on the other hand, have orange flesh and a sweet flavor, especially when roasted. Yams are commonly used in...you guessed it: sweet potato casserole.

LIBATION RECOMMENDATION

Look no further than a classic Jack and Coke for this menu...or Jack and Diet if you're watching your figure.

EFFICIENCY TIP

Since the "fries" take the longest, get them in the oven first, before you start chopping or cooking anything else. They'll be getting done just as you're building your Little Macs. Then you can keep them warm in a 200°F oven until you're ready to serve.

Little Macs with Very, Very Special Sauce

One 15-ounce can black or green lentils, drained
1½ teaspoons smoked paprika
½ teaspoon onion powder
½ teaspoon garlic powder
⅛ teaspoon pepper
1 tablespoon low-sodium tamari
1 teaspoon vegan Worcestershire sauce
¼ cup plus 1 tablespoon vital wheat gluten
2 tablespoons extra-virgin olive oil
16 small slices vegan cheddar cheeze
8 tiny sesame seed buns (about 2 inches wide) plus the bottom halves of 8 other tiny buns (to use as the middle bun)
½ cup Very, Very Special Sauce (recipe follows)
2 cups shredded romaine lettuce
2 small dill pickles, thinly sliced
½ cup minced white onion
8 long toothpicks or skewers

To make the burger patties, in a medium bowl, combine the lentils, paprika, onion powder, garlic powder, pepper, tamari, and Worcestershire. Mash it all together with a fork or your hands until about 70 percent of the lentils are mashed. Add the wheat gluten and continue mashing until there are no dry parts remaining and you have a ball of dough. Scoop out a heaping tablespoon of dough and place it on a large cutting board or other work surface. Repeat until you have 16 lumps of dough. Roll each lump into a ball, then flatten it into a 2-inch patty.

In a large skillet, heat the olive oil to medium-high, and add the patties (you may have to fry them in two shifts). Fry on one side for

about 5 minutes, or until browned. Then flip, top each patty with a cheddar slice, and fry for another 5 minutes.

In the meantime, get your tiny buns ready. Slather the top and bottom bun halves, and one side of the middle buns, with the Very, Very Special Sauce.

By now your patties should be ready, so it's time to start assembling. Place one patty on each of the bottom bun halves. Top the patties with half of the lettuce and half of the pickles. Place the middle bun pieces, sauce side down, on top of that, followed by the remaining patties, lettuce, and pickles, and the onion. Finally, cover with the bun tops and use toothpicks or skewers to hold them together.

VERY, VERY SPECIAL SAUCE

1 cup vegan mayo
½ cup sweet pickle relish
½ cup ketchup
¼ cup yellow mustard

In a small bowl, whisk all this stuff together.

Baked Sweet Potato "Fries" with Adobo Dipping Sauce

2 large sweet potatoes, cut into ½-inch-thick wedges
2 teaspoons extra-virgin olive oil
½ teaspoon smoked paprika
¼ teaspoon ground coriander
¼ teaspoon ground cumin
¼ teaspoon salt
Pinch of pepper
Adobo Dipping Sauce (recipe follows)

Preheat the oven to 350°F. Line a baking sheet with parchment paper or a Silpat baking mat. In a medium bowl, combine the sweet potatoes, oil, paprika, coriander, cumin, salt, and pepper, and toss until the sweet potatoes are well coated. Spread out the sweet potatoes in a single layer on the baking sheet. Roast for 45 to 50 minutes, or until cooked through and browned. Keep them warm in a 200°F oven until ready to serve. Serve with Adobo Dipping Sauce.

ADOBO DIPPING SAUCE

¼ cup ketchup
1½ cups vegan mayo
½ teaspoon fresh lime juice
1 teaspoon adobo sauce (see WTF below)

In a small bowl, whisk all this stuff together.

WTF is adobo sauce? It's that thick, deep red sauce that canned chipotle peppers are packed in. It's spicy with a great smoky flavor, and it usually comes in a 7-ounce can labeled "Chipotle Peppers in Adobo Sauce."

SHOPPING LIST

The Happiest Meal

PRODUCE

- Lime (1)
- Romaine lettuce (1 head)
- Sweet potatoes (2 large)
- White onion (1 small)

PANTRY

- Vital wheat gluten (¼ cup plus 1 tablespoon)
- Black or green lentils (one 15-ounce can)
- Chipotle peppers in adobo sauce (one 7-ounce can)
- Dill pickles (2 small)
- Sweet pickle relish (½ cup)
- Extra-virgin olive oil (2 tablespoons plus 2 teaspoons)
- Tamari, low-sodium (1 tablespoon)
- Vegan Worcestershire sauce (1 teaspoon)
- Ketchup (¾ cup)
- Yellow mustard (¼ cup)
- Ground coriander (¼ teaspoon)
- Ground cumin (¼ teaspoon)
- Garlic powder (½ teaspoon)
- Onion powder (½ teaspoon)
- Smoked paprika (2 teaspoons)
- Salt
- Pepper

MISCELLANEOUS

- Vegan cheddar cheeze (8 ounces)
- Vegan mayo (2½ cups)
- Tiny sesame seed buns (about 2 inches wide) (16)
- Long toothpicks or skewers (8)

14 LITTLE TOKYO

U-NO-gi Nigiri with Kabayaki Sauce

Sautéed Green Beans

Blackened Edamame

Shopping List

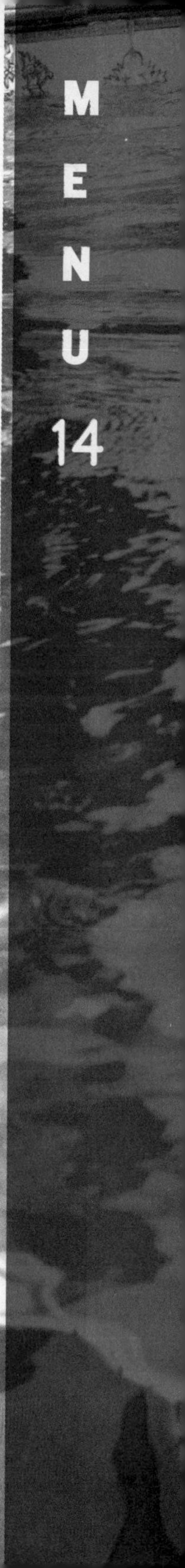

When I gave up animal products, sushi was the thing that I missed the most. And one of my favorite ingredients was eel, or "unagi." Sweet, smoky, and a little crisp around the edges — what's not to like? Oh, right, it's a gross slippery eel. Well, those were the days before I made the connection with my food and where it came from. Anyway, the great thing about being awesome is that I possess the power to create similar flavors and textures without using animals, which is what I've done here.

LIBATION RECOMMENDATION

Go with the Nashitini (see recipe, page 197). It's a crowd-pleaser for sure.

EFFICIENCY TIP

The kabayaki sauce can be made way ahead of time and stored in the fridge, or it can be store-bought. You can even go so far as to visit your nearest sushi restaurant and ask them to make you a bunch of the little formed rice balls to take home. I've done that. If do you choose to make your own rice, while the rice is cooking, cook the mushrooms, transfer them to a plate, and cover with foil to keep warm. Use the same boiling water to blanch the green beans and the edamame. Begin sautéing the green beans and edamame at the same time. The edamame cook faster, so serve those first, then bring out the green beans. While your guests are fawning over your first two dishes, you can put together the nigiri. And just as their praise is starting to dwindle, you triumphantly emerge from the kitchen with the nigiri on a platter to a standing ovation. It's all about the showmanship.

U-NO-gi Nigiri with Kabayaki Sauce

1 tablespoon low-sodium tamari, plus more for serving

2 teaspoons maple syrup

2 drops liquid smoke (see WTF below)

3 teaspoons canola oil

2 portobello mushrooms, stemmed

1 teaspoon sesame oil

2 cups cooked sushi rice (recipe follows)

1 or 2 sheets nori, cut into sixteen 4-inch-by-½-inch strips

¼ cup store-bought kabayaki sauce or Sexy Kabayaki Sauce (recipe follows, page 132)

Sesame seeds, for garnish

Wasabi paste, for serving

Scan to watch the video.

In a large bowl, whisk together 1 tablespoon tamari, the maple syrup, liquid smoke, and 1 teaspoon of the canola oil, then add the mushrooms and toss to coat. In a medium skillet, heat the remaining 2 teaspoons canola oil over medium heat. Place the mushrooms, gill side up, in the pan, and sear for 3 to 4 minutes, or until browned. Flip the mushrooms, and drizzle the sesame oil over the tops. Cook for 3 to 4 more minutes, until the mushrooms are cooked all the way through. Let cool.

While the mushrooms are cooling, take a little bit of the sushi rice and form it into an oblong ball about the size of a thumb. Make 16 of these.

When the mushrooms are cool enough to handle, cut each one into 8 pieces — make 4 slices on a slight bias, then cut those slices in half crosswise. Place

WTF is liquid smoke? It is an extremely powerful flavoring made from natural hickory smoke. It comes in a small bottle, and you only need a little drop to get big flavor. Oftentimes people have a dedicated eyedropper for adding it to recipes. You can find it near the barbecue sauces in any grocery store, or on the Interwebs.

a mushroom piece on top of each rice thumb (which is what I'm calling them now), and wrap a nori strip around it, making sure the seam is on the bottom. Wet the tip of your finger with water and moisten the nori strip at the seam to help it stay closed. Brush the mushrooms with the kabayaki sauce and garnish with sesame seeds. Serve with wasabi and tamari.

SUSHI RICE

1 cup sushi rice (see WTF below)

1⅛ cups water

2 tablespoons rice vinegar

1 teaspoon agave nectar

1 teaspoon mirin

1 teaspoon salt

In a bowl, cover the rice with water. Mix it around with your hand until the water becomes milky white. Drain and rinse until the water runs clear. In a heavy-bottomed pot, bring the rice and 1⅛ cups water to a boil over medium heat, then cover. Let boil for 1 minute, then reduce the heat to low, and cook for 16 to 18 minutes, or until the water is completely absorbed. Remove the pot from the heat, keep the rice covered, and allow it to cool for 12 to 15 minutes.

In a small bowl, whisk together the vinegar, agave nectar, mirin, and salt. Turn the warm rice out onto a wide plate

> **WTF** is sushi rice? Sushi rice is made with short-grain Japanese rice (or japonica rice) and flavored with a sweetened vinegar mixture. You can find it in a Japanese market or Asian section of the grocery store, and it's usually called "sushi rice."

or casserole, and with a broad wooden spoon, gently fold in the vinegar mixture. Continue this folding motion for several minutes, and with your nonfolding hand, fan the rice with a newspaper or something else fan-like to help it cool quickly. Do not put the rice in the fridge, as that will kill its flavor and its all-important sticky properties. Continue the fanning and folding process until the rice gets to room temperature. Now it's ready to use.

SEXY KABAYAKI SAUCE

½ cup low-sodium tamari

½ cup mirin

¼ cup unrefined granulated sugar

In a small saucepan, combine all the ingredients and bring to a simmer over medium-high heat. Simmer, stirring continuously, for about 5 minutes, or until the sugar is dissolved and the sauce has thickened. Let cool. Store any unused sauce in an airtight container in the fridge for up to 2 weeks; you can add it to a stir-fry or use it to dress a cold noodle salad.

Sautéed Green Beans

1 pound green beans, trimmed
2 teaspoons canola oil
4 garlic cloves, grated
One ½-inch piece fresh ginger, peeled and grated
2 teaspoons mirin
2 teaspoons low-sodium tamari
Salt and pepper
½ teaspoon sesame oil
Healthy pinch of sesame seeds

Bring a medium pot of salted water to a boil. Have an ice bath standing by. Drop the green beans into the boiling water, and blanch for 2 minutes. Remove the green beans from the boiling water and submerge in the ice bath immediately. Once the green beans are cool, drain and pat dry with a clean kitchen towel or paper towels.

In a large skillet, heat the canola oil over medium-high heat. In a medium bowl, combine the green beans, garlic, ginger, mirin, and tamari and toss until the green beans are well coated. Remove the green beans from the bowl, allowing the excess liquid to fall away, and place them in the skillet. Sauté for 1 to 2 minutes, or until browned on one side. Then toss and sauté for 1 to 2 more minutes to brown the other side. Season with salt and pepper to taste, and add the sesame oil and sesame seeds. Toss one more time and remove from the pan. Serve hot.

Blackened Edamame

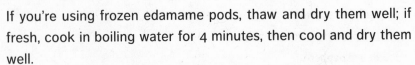

1 pound fresh or frozen edamame pods

Togarashi seasoning (see WTF below), or salt, pepper, and sesame seeds, for garnish

If you're using frozen edamame pods, thaw and dry them well; if fresh, cook in boiling water for 4 minutes, then cool and dry them well.

Heat a large skillet over high heat. Place the edamame pods in the dry pan, and sear for 4 to 5 minutes, or until there are blackened spots on one side. Then toss and cook for 4 to 5 more minutes, or until there are blackened spots on the other side. Transfer to a serving bowl and sprinkle with togarashi seasoning. Serve in a bowl, with a second bowl for the discarded pods.

WTF is togarashi seasoning? It is a combination of dried and ground Japanese chile peppers that packs great flavor and a good amount of heat. You'll have to get this at a Japanese market or on the Interwebs.

Little Tokyo

SHOPPING LIST

PRODUCE

Portobello mushrooms (2)
Green beans (1 pound)
Edamame pods, fresh or frozen (1 pound)
Garlic (4 cloves)
Ginger (one ½-inch piece)

PANTRY

Maple syrup (2 teaspoons)
Agave nectar (1 teaspoon)
Canola oil (5 teaspoons)
Liquid smoke (2 drops)
Sesame seeds (about 1 tablespoon)
Salt
Pepper

ASIAN AISLE/MARKET

Sushi rice (1 cup)
Nori (1 or 2 sheets)
Togarashi seasoning (optional; for garnish)
Wasabi paste (about ¼ cup)
Sesame oil (1½ teaspoons)
Rice vinegar (2 tablespoons)
Mirin (1 tablespoon)
Tamari, low-sodium (½ cup)
Kabayaki sauce (¼ cup) — OR if you want to make my Sexy Kabayaki Sauce, you'll need:
- Unrefined granulated sugar (¼ cup)
- Mirin (½ cup)
- Tamari, low-sodium (½ cup)

15

SATAY-DAY NIGHT FEVER

Tempeh Satay with Peanut Sauce

Grilled Baby Bok Choy

Teriyaki Almonds

Shopping List

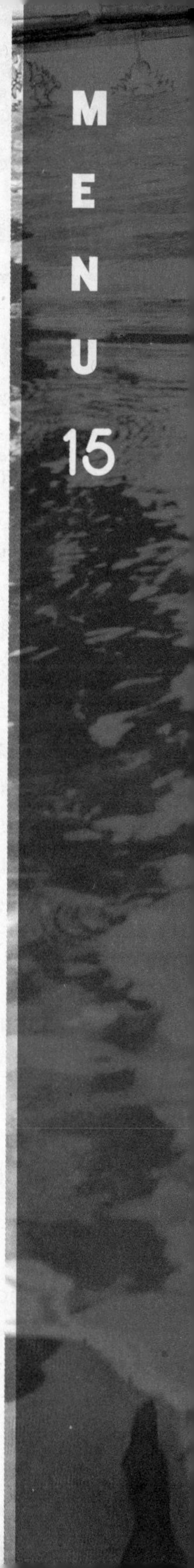

MENU 15

Using the same sauce in several dishes is a great time-saving technique that I made up just for you and this book. Okay, maybe I didn't make it up, but it's a perfect technique for an efficiently prepared happy hour.

LIBATION RECOMMENDATION

The Punchy Pineapple (see recipe, page 191) is a great complement to the teriyaki flavors in these dishes.

EFFICIENCY TIP

Get the almonds in the oven first so they have a chance to cool. While the tempeh is boiling, grill the bok choy and place it in an oven-safe vessel covered with foil. Once the almonds come out of the oven, reduce the temperature to its lowest setting and put the bok choy in there to keep warm. Serve the almonds as soon as they're cool, and then serve the satay and bok choy together.

Tempeh Satay with Peanut Sauce

Two 8-ounce packages tempeh, cut into 3- to 4-inch slices, each about ½ inch thick
½ cup low-sodium tamari
¼ cup mirin
3 garlic cloves, crushed
1 thumb-size piece ginger, peeled and sliced
3½ cups water
½ cup arrowroot
½ cup rice flour
1 cup panko bread crumbs
½ cup sweetened coconut shreds
Salt and pepper
2 tablespoons canola or other neutral-flavored oil
16 wooden skewers
Sesame seeds, for garnish
Lime wedges, for garnish
1½ cups store-bought peanut sauce or Sexy Peanut Sauce (recipe follows)

In a medium pot, combine the tempeh slices, tamari, mirin, garlic, ginger, and 3 cups of the water, and bring to simmer over medium-high heat. Simmer for 15 minutes, until the tempeh has softened somewhat. Then remove them from the pot with a slotted spoon and set aside to cool.

Once the tempeh is cooked, set up your breading station. In a medium bowl, whisk together the remaining ½ cup water and the arrowroot. Spread out the rice flour on a large plate. On another large plate, mix together the bread crumbs and coconut, and season with salt and pepper. Line a baking sheet with parchment paper or a Silpat baking mat so that you have somewhere to place the breaded tempeh. To bread the tempeh, roll the tempeh slices in the flour, then dunk them in the arrowroot slurry, then coat them in the bread crumbs–coconut mixture. Place them on the baking sheet.

In a large skillet, heat the oil over medium-high heat. Working in batches, brown the tempeh on each side, turning with tongs after 2 or 3 minutes. When browned, remove from the pan to allow to cool slightly. When they are cool enough to handle, skewer the slices lengthwise. Arrange sexily on a fancy-ass plate, and garnish with the sesame seeds and lime wedges. Serve with the peanut sauce for dipping.

SEXY PEANUT SAUCE

½ cup coconut milk
½ cup smooth peanut butter
2 teaspoons low-sodium tamari
½ teaspoon Sriracha or other Thai chili sauce
2 teaspoons fresh lime juice
¼ cup water
Salt and pepper

In a medium bowl, whisk together the coconut milk, peanut butter, tamari, Sriracha, lime juice, and water until smooth. Season with salt and pepper to taste.

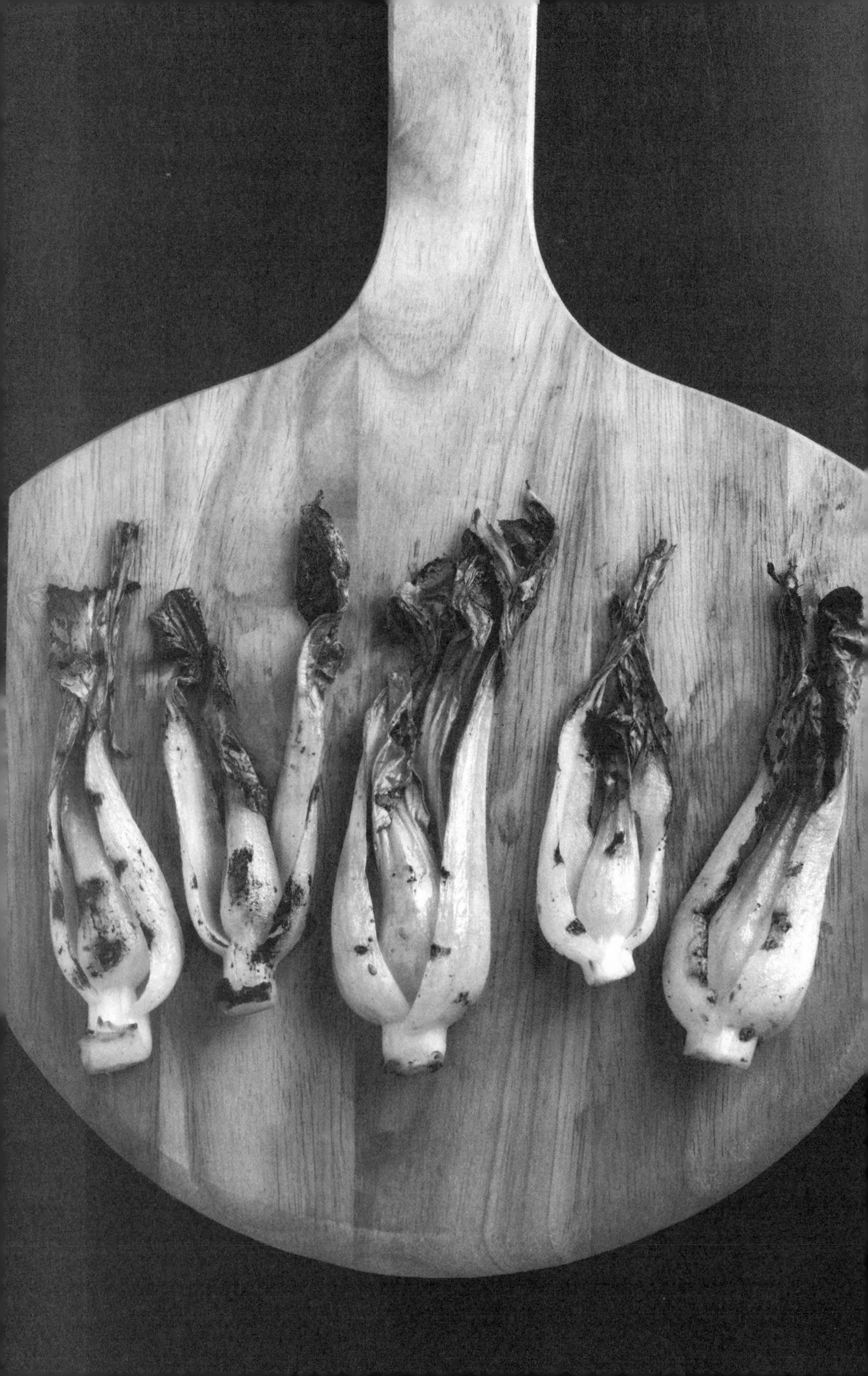

Grilled Baby Bok Choy

6 heads baby bok choy, halved and large leaves (if any) removed

½ cup teriyaki sauce

Heat the grill or a grill pan to medium. In a large bowl, toss the bok choy with the teriyaki sauce. Let it marinate on the counter for 10 to 15 minutes while your grill heats up.

Remove the bok choy from the marinade, allowing the excess marinade to fall away and reserving it for drizzling. Place the bok choy, cut sides down, on the grill. Grill the bok choy, leaving it as is, for 5 to 6 minutes, or until there are some nice grill marks. Flip it and grill the other side for 6 to 8 more minutes. It should be slightly tender but still have some firmness. Arrange the bok choy on a plate and drizzle any remaining marinade over it. Serve warm or at room temperature.

Teriyaki Almonds

2 cups roasted unsalted almonds

¼ cup teriyaki sauce

2 teaspoons sesame seeds

2 teaspoons rice flour

½ teaspoon salt

Preheat the oven to 300°F. Line 1 or 2 baking sheets with parchment paper or Silpat baking mats. In a medium bowl, combine all the ingredients and toss until the almonds are well coated. Spread out the almonds in a single layer on the baking sheets. Roast for 15 minutes. Remove from the oven and let cool.

SHOPPING LIST

Satay-day Night Fever

PRODUCE

- Lime (1)
- Baby bok choy (6 heads)
- Garlic (3 cloves)
- Ginger (1 thumb-size piece)

PANTRY

- Rice flour (½ cup plus 2 teaspoons)
- Arrowroot (½ cup)
- Sweetened coconut shreds (½ cup)
- Canola or other neutral-flavored oil (2 tablespoons)
- Almonds, roasted unsalted (2 cups)
- Sesame seeds (2 teaspoons, plus more for garnish)
- Salt
- Pepper

ASIAN AISLE/MARKET

- Panko bread crumbs (1 cup)
- Mirin (¼ cup)
- Tamari, low-sodium (½ cup)
- Teriyaki sauce (6 fluid ounces [¾ cup])
- Peanut sauce (12 fluid ounces [1½ cups]) — OR if you want to make my Sexy Peanut Sauce, you'll need:
  - Lime (1)
  - Smooth peanut butter (½ cup)
  - Tamari, low-sodium (2 teaspoons)
  - Sriracha or other Thai chili sauce (½ teaspoon)
  - Coconut milk (½ cup)

MISCELLANEOUS

- Tempeh (two 8-ounce packages)
- Wooden skewers (16)

16

STATE FAIR FARE

Man, do I hate the fair. Always have. Even before I was clued in on animal suffering and vegan stuff, I still avoided the fair like the plague. My friends would always be like, "Hey, let's go to the fair!" And I'd be like, "Let me get this straight: You want me to walk around all day in some filthy, stinky farmland and throw some balls and rings at stuff, so I can win shitty, useless prizes that I have to carry around all day and will end up throwing away when I get home? And then I'm going to eat so much sausage, hot dogs, and funnel cake — which, at first, I'll enjoy — until I have to take three separate dumps in Porta-Johns, before we spend an hour finding our car and another hour getting out of the parking lot? That's how you'll have me spending my Saturday? I don't even care if Warrant is opening for Stryper! No, thank you!"

Just because I hate the fair, though, doesn't mean I hate the food. I love the food. And corn dogs are at the top of the list.

P.S. Wow! I just went and watched a Stryper video, and I recommend you do the same. You will not be disappointed.

LIBATION RECOMMENDATION

Since we're dealing with some extremely, ahem, casual food here, I'd pair it with a Starburst (see recipe, page 201)...reminds me of candy and junk food, perfect for the fair.

EFFICIENCY TIP

Start by prepping the Okra "Fries" and getting them in the oven. Then make the sauces, and continue on to the Corn Dawggie process. Once the Okra "Fries" are done, remove them from the oven and let them hang out on the counter. When you start frying the Corn Dawggies, put the okra back in the oven for a few minutes to reheat. Then serve everything at once.

Corn Dawggies with the Most Wonderful Ketchup

Canola, vegetable, or any other high-heat oil, for deep-frying

½ cup unbleached all-purpose flour

½ cup cornmeal

½ teaspoon ancho chile powder

¼ teaspoon smoked paprika

½ teaspoon salt

2 teaspoons unrefined granulated sugar

2 teaspoons baking powder

⅔ cup unsweetened nondairy milk

½ cup arrowroot

4 veggie dogs, cut into thirds

Toothpicks

Yellow or whole-grain mustard, for serving

The Most Wonderful Ketchup (recipe follows), for serving

Pour oil to a depth of 3 inches into a pot, high-sided pan, or deep fryer. Line a plate with paper towels and set it next to the stove. Heat the oil over medium heat until it registers 375°F on a deep-frying thermometer. In a medium bowl, combine the flour, cornmeal, chile powder, paprika, salt, sugar, and baking powder. Stir in the nondairy milk and keep stirring until you have a batter that is slightly thicker than pancake batter. Let rest for at least 5 minutes.

Spread out the arrowroot on a large plate. Working in batches, roll the veggie dogs in the arrowroot until completely coated, tapping the dogs to remove the excess, and immerse the dogs in the batter. Using a fork or chopsticks, take the dogs out of the batter and gently lower them into the oil. Fry for 3 to 5 minutes, or until golden on all sides, making sure to turn them a few times for even cooking. Transfer the dogs to the paper towel–lined plate. When they're cool enough to handle, cut them in half crosswise, and serve with toothpicks, mustard, and the Most Wonderful Ketchup.

THE MOST WONDERFUL KETCHUP

1 cup ketchup

2 teaspoons pomegranate concentrate (see WTF below)

½ teaspoon agave nectar

Whisk all this stuff together in a bowl.

WTF is pomegranate concentrate? WHAT it is, is pretty self-explanatory, but WHERE to find it might be a little more of a mystery. You can find it at supplement and vitamin stores, and if all else fails, the Interwebs come to the rescue.

Okra "Fries" with White Barbecue Sauce

½ pound okra, trimmed and halved lengthwise

1 tablespoon extra-virgin olive oil

¼ cup cornmeal

Salt and pepper

White Barbecue Sauce (recipe follows), for serving

Preheat the oven to 450°F. Line 2 baking sheets with parchment paper or Silpat baking mats. In a medium bowl, toss the okra with the olive oil, cornmeal, and salt and pepper to taste. Spread out the okra in a single layer on the baking sheets. Bake for 13 to 15 minutes, or until browned and crisp. Serve warm with White Barbecue Sauce.

WHITE BARBECUE SAUCE

Seriously, WTF is white barbecue sauce?!? It's a tangy, mayo-based sauce invented in Alabama for brushing on grilled foods during the last few minutes of cooking. It can also be served on the side as a condiment. It's also what comes out of Paula Deen if you prick her with a pin. Disclaimer: Do not prick Paula Deen with anything. Thank you.

½ cup vegan mayo

4 teaspoons apple cider vinegar

½ teaspoon agave nectar

1 teaspoon prepared horseradish

½ teaspoon smoked paprika

Salt and pepper

In a small bowl, whisk together the mayo, vinegar, agave nectar, horseradish, and paprika. Season with salt and pepper to taste.

State Fair Fare

PRODUCE

Okra (½ pound)

PANTRY

Unbleached all-purpose flour (½ cup)
Unrefined granulated sugar (2 teaspoons)
Cornmeal (¾ cup)
Baking powder (2 teaspoons)
Arrowroot (½ cup)
Agave nectar (1 teaspoon)
Pomegranate concentrate (2 teaspoons)
Canola, vegetable, or any other high-heat oil (1 to 2 quarts, depending on the size of your deep-frying vessel)
Extra-virgin olive oil (1 tablespoon)
Apple cider vinegar (4 teaspoons)
Ketchup (1 cup)
Yellow or whole-grain mustard (for serving)
Prepared horseradish (1 teaspoon)
Ancho chile powder (½ teaspoon)
Smoked paprika (¾ teaspoon)
Salt
Pepper

MISCELLANEOUS

Nondairy milk, unsweetened (⅔ cup)
Vegan mayo (½ cup)
Veggie dogs (4)
Toothpicks

17

GLENNTIL TAMALE BITES

Tamale Bites with Fresh Tomatillo Salsa and Avocado-Walnut Puree

Cumin-Scented Chard

Tortillas Dulces

Shopping List

I have a friend. His name is Glenn. A few years back, my friends and I went on a camping trip to Montana, and on this trip someone came up with the bright idea of working the name Glenn into famous people's names and other words. It just worked too well: Glennifer Aniston, Jimmy Glenndrix, Glennard Nimoy, Harry and the Glenndersons, Glenntil Soup, and, my personal favorite, Glennjaglenn Frankglenn. Years later, and we're still coming up with new ones. So the great Crandall, my former cameraman and contributor of the epic belch you hear at the end of each *Sexy Vegan* episode, developed a website as a way to collect the terms that we came up with. If you have a friend named Glenn, go to UrGlenndictionary.com for a good start on Glennded terms. You can even submit your own. If you don't have a friend named Glenn, go find one — it'll be worth it.

Anyway, I really love tamales, but they are rather laborious, and not fit for a happy hour situation. As douchey as I feel saying it, these would be more like (gulp) "deconstructed" tamales. Blech…now I have to go wash my mouth out.

LIBATION RECOMMENDATION

A Bloody Vulcan (see recipe, page 193) is perfect for this menu, since you've already got tomatillos, but you could also go with a Pomarita (see recipe, page 203) and be perfectly happy (and drunk).

EFFICIENCY TIP

Get the polenta in the oven first, then chop up everything that needs to be chopped up. Cook the lentil mixture and the chard at the same time. While they're cooking, completely prepare the tortillas dulces, up until they're about to be baked. When the lentils and chard are done, turn off the heat and put the lids on their respective vessels. Now, make the salsa and walnut puree (you can also make them the day before as a super–time saver), and then reheat the chard and lentils for a couple of minutes before serving. Just before you walk out of the kitchen with your glorious platter of goodies, put the tortillas dulces in the oven, and set your timer so you don't forget about them.

Tamale Bites with Fresh Tomatillo Salsa and Avocado-Walnut Puree

One 20-ounce prepared polenta in a tube (see WTF below), cut into twelve ½-inch-thick rounds

2 teaspoons extra-virgin olive oil, plus more for brushing

Salt and pepper

½ cup diced yellow onion

1 jalapeño pepper, seeded and diced

4 garlic cloves, minced

4 teaspoons chili powder

2 teaspoons ground cumin

Two 15-ounce cans lentils, drained

4 teaspoons tomato paste

2 cups vegetable stock

Fresh Tomatillo Salsa (recipe follows), for serving

Avocado-Walnut Puree (recipe follows), for serving

WTF is "polenta in a tube"? It's prepared polenta packaged in plastic in the form of a fat sausage-like cylinder. It's nice and firm, so you can cut it into rounds. If you can't find prepared polenta in your grocery store, do not panic. As long as you know how to boil water, you're cool. Bring 3 cups salted water to a boil over high heat, and whisk in 1 cup cornmeal. Reduce the heat to low and continue whisking for a few minutes. Cook for 15 minutes, or until the polenta is thickened. Pour it into a greased-up casserole, and let it completely cool. You can now cut it into squares or whatever shape you like, then proceed with the recipe. You can make the polenta a day ahead of time if you like.

Preheat the oven to 400°F. Line a baking sheet with parchment paper or a Silpat baking mat. Brush both sides of each polenta round with oil, and season with salt and pepper. Place the rounds on the baking sheet. Bake for 20 minutes, or until slightly browned around the edges. Turn off the oven, leaving the polenta in there to keep warm.

In a large skillet, heat 2 teaspoons olive oil over medium heat. Add the onion, jalapeño, and a pinch of salt, and cook for 5 minutes. Add the garlic, and cook for 2 minutes. Add the chili powder, cumin, and lentils. Stir that all together, and cook for 1 minute. Then add the tomato paste and vegetable stock, and bring to a simmer. Simmer for 5 minutes, then mash some of the lentils until the mixture thickens into a stew-like consistency.

To serve, top the polenta rounds with the lentil mixture, Fresh Tomatillo Salsa, and Avocado-Walnut Puree.

FRESH TOMATILLO SALSA

½ pound tomatillos, husks removed, rinsed, and quartered
½ jalapeño pepper, seeded
½ medium yellow onion, roughly chopped
1 garlic clove
½ packed cup fresh cilantro leaves
1 teaspoon fresh lime juice
1 teaspoon agave nectar
Salt and pepper

In a food processor or blender, puree the tomatillos, jalapeño, onion, garlic, cilantro, lime juice, and agave nectar until smooth. Season with salt and pepper to taste.

AVOCADO-WALNUT PUREE

1 large avocado, roughly chopped
½ cup raw walnuts

¼ cup water

1 teaspoon fresh lime juice

¼ teaspoon ground cumin

¼ teaspoon ground coriander

Salt and pepper

In a food processor or blender, puree the avocado, walnuts, water, lime juice, cumin, and coriander until smooth. Season with salt and pepper to taste.

Cumin-Scented Chard

2 teaspoons extra-virgin olive oil

½ teaspoon cumin seeds

½ teaspoon coriander seeds

4 garlic cloves, thinly sliced

2 bunches red chard, leaves roughly chopped and thicker parts of the stalks sliced into ½-inch pieces

2 beefsteak tomatoes, cut into bite-size chunks

Salt

2 cups vegetable stock

1 teaspoon sherry vinegar

Pepper

2 tablespoons pepitas (see WTF below)

In a large pot (with a lid), heat the olive oil over medium-high heat. Add the cumin and coriander seeds, and cook for 2 to 3 minutes, or until they start popping and crackling. Add the garlic, and cook for 2 to 3 minutes, or until the edges begin to slightly brown. Stir in the chard leaves, chard stems, tomatoes, and a healthy pinch of salt, and cook for 3 to 4 more minutes. Add the vegetable stock and vinegar, and reduce the heat to medium. Cover the pot and simmer for 8 minutes, stirring occasionally. Uncover the pot, and continue cooking for 3 to 4 minutes, or until most of the liquid evaporates. Season with salt and pepper to taste, and garnish with pepitas.

WTF is a pepita? A pepita is the hulled and usually roasted kernel of a pumpkin seed. You can find pepitas in the Mexican aisle of most grocery stores.

Tortillas Dulces

Four 6-inch flour tortillas, quartered

¼ cup melted vegan margarine

½ teaspoon ground cinnamon

2 tablespoons unrefined granulated sugar

Powdered sugar, for garnish

Dark chocolate bar, for garnish

Preheat the oven to 400°F. Line a baking sheet with parchment paper or a Silpat baking mat. Brush both sides of the tortillas with the margarine and place them on the baking sheet.

In a small bowl, stir together the cinnamon and granulated sugar. Sprinkle the top of each tortilla with the cinnamon-sugar mixture. Bake for 6 to 8 minutes, or until crisp. Remove from the oven to let cool.

When the tortillas dulces are cool enough to handle, arrange them sexily on some sort of platter. Dust with powdered sugar, and with a zester or grater, shave the dark chocolate on top to your heart's desire.

Glenntil Tamale Bites

SHOPPING LIST

PRODUCE

Lime (1)
Beefsteak tomatoes (2)
Tomatillos (½ pound)
Avocado (1 large)
Jalapeño peppers (2)
Red chard (2 bunches)
Yellow onion (1)
Garlic (9 cloves)
Cilantro (1 bunch)

PANTRY

Unrefined granulated sugar (2 tablespoons)
Powdered sugar (for garnish)
Prepared polenta (one 20-ounce tube)
Lentils (two 15-ounce cans)
Tomato paste (4 teaspoons)
Vegetable stock (32 fluid ounces [4 cups])
Agave nectar (1 teaspoon)
Extra-virgin olive oil (4 teaspoons, plus more for brushing)
Sherry vinegar (1 teaspoon)
Walnuts, raw (½ cup)
Pepitas (2 tablespoons)
Chili powder (4 teaspoons)
Ground cinnamon (½ teaspoon)
Coriander seeds (½ teaspoon)
Ground coriander (¼ teaspoon)
Ground cumin (2¼ teaspoons)
Cumin seeds (½ teaspoon)
Salt
Pepper

MISCELLANEOUS

Vegan margarine (¼ cup)
Dark chocolate bar (for garnish)
Flour tortillas, 6-inch (4)

18 K-TOWN

Bello Bulgogi

Chapchae

Shopping List

With my days of Korean barbecue joints behind me, I still have a periodic hankering for Korean fare. And even though "bibimbap" is superfun to say, I opted to veganize bulgogi beef. Not quite as fun to say out loud, but there are fewer components, there are a lot of flavors going on, and it's wrapped in lettuce leaves, which makes it perfect happy hour grub. Being able to eat your utensil is my favorite thing in the world. Of all things in this life, THAT is my favorite. Weird, huh?

LIBATION RECOMMENDATION

I created the Nashitini (see recipe, page 197) for this menu, as oftentimes this dish is served with sliced or grated nashi pears. I was more in the mood to mix them with sake and drink them ...shocker.

EFFICIENCY TIP

The longer you marinate the mushrooms, the better, so do that in the morning. The rest of the menu comes together pretty quickly.

Bello Bulgogi

Bulgogi Marinade

1½ cups low-sodium tamari

¼ cup plus 2 tablespoons brown sugar

3 tablespoons sesame oil

6 garlic cloves, grated

2 thumb-size pieces fresh ginger, peeled and grated

½ teaspoon chile flakes

4 scallions, thinly sliced

6 portobello mushrooms, stemmed and cut into ½-inch-thick slices

1 tablespoon extra-virgin olive oil

1 medium yellow onion, thinly sliced

1 large carrot, cut into matchsticks

Salt and pepper

1 tablespoon toasted sesame seeds

1 head leafy lettuce (romaine, red leaf, butter), leaves separated

Kimchi, for serving

To make the marinade, in a large measuring cup or bowl, combine the tamari, brown sugar, sesame oil, garlic, ginger, chile flakes, and scallions. Whisk until the sugar is dissolved.

Place the sliced mushrooms in a large zip-top bag (you might need 2 bags). Pour the marinade over the mushrooms, and gently slosh them around so they get coated. Squeeze the bag to suck out as much air as possible, and zip it closed. Put the bag in the fridge to let the mushrooms marinate for at least 2 hours or up to 8 hours, turning every so often to ensure even marination.

In a large skillet, heat the olive oil over medium-high heat. Add the onion and carrot and cook for 3 to 4 minutes, or until they start to become tender. In the meantime, remove the mushrooms from the marinade, letting the excess marinade fall away. Be sure to keep the marinade, as you'll need it for the Chapchae (see recipe, page 166). Add the mushrooms to the skillet, and cook, stirring occasionally, for 6 to 8 minutes, or until cooked through. Season with salt and pepper to taste, stir in the sesame seeds, turn off the heat, and cover to keep warm until serving.

To serve, make little "tacos" with the portobellos, using the lettuce leaves as the wrap. Top with a bit of kimchi.

Chapchae

6 ounces bean thread noodles (see WTF below)

1 teaspoon extra-virgin olive oil

1 large carrot, cut into matchsticks

1 medium zucchini, cut into matchsticks

¾ pound baby spinach

½ cup Bulgogi Marinade (see Bello Bulgogi recipe, page 164)

Salt and pepper

Bring a large pot of water to a boil. The noodles will most likely be in 3 tight bunches; drop them into the water. Return the water to a boil, and cook for about 6 minutes, stirring often to prevent stickage. When the noodles become translucent and you can bite into one easily, they are done. Drain the noodles and rinse under cold running water to stop the cooking, and drain again. The noodles can be very long, so roughly chop them with a pair of kitchen shears or a chef's knife. Set aside.

In a large skillet, heat the oil over medium-high heat. Add the carrot and zucchini, and sauté for 3 to 4 minutes, or until slightly brown. Add the spinach, and cook for 2 to 3 minutes, or until the spinach is wilted. Finally, add the noodles and the marinade. Toss everything together and cook for 2 to 3 minutes, or until the marinade is reduced by half and everything is well coated and combined. Season with salt and pepper to taste. Serve hot, warm, or at room temperature.

WTF are bean thread noodles? They can be made from mung beans or yams and are also called glass noodles or cellophane noodles. You can find them in an Asian market for sure, and possibly in the Asian aisle of your regular grocery store. If all else fails, the Interwebs come to the rescue.

SHOPPING LIST

K-Town

PRODUCE

- Portobello mushrooms (6)
- Carrots (2 large)
- Leafy lettuce (romaine, red leaf, butter) (1 head)
- Zucchini (1)
- Baby spinach (¾ pound)
- Scallions (1 bunch)
- Yellow onion (1 medium)
- Garlic (6 cloves)
- Ginger (2 thumb-size pieces)

PANTRY

- Brown sugar (¼ cup plus 2 tablespoons)
- Extra-virgin olive oil (1 tablespoon plus 1 teaspoon)
- Chile flakes (½ teaspoon)
- Sesame seeds (1 tablespoon)
- Salt
- Pepper

ASIAN AISLE/MARKET

- Kimchi (one 14-ounce jar)
- Bean thread noodles (6 ounces)
- Sesame oil (3 tablespoons)
- Tamari, low-sodium (1½ cups)

19

BOMBERS AND BREAD BOWLS

Spinach-Artichoke Dip

Braised Broccoli Rabe

Shaved Cantaloupe
with Pine Nut–Basil Cream

Shopping List

Running a close second to edible utensils as my favorite things in the world are edible bowls. And this dip is served in one. I used to go to a local place called BJ's when I was in college, and it had something called Bongo Bongo Dip — its signature creamy, cheesy artichoke and spinach dip. I wanted to re-create it as best I could, and I think this version is even better.

BJ's also served a drink called the BJ's Bomber. It came in a giant chalice and contained eleven shots of various alcohols and a splash of a sugary fruit juice — all poured over ice. That's all for one person. It had a round slice of orange floating on top of it, which was piled with sugar and set ablaze with Bacardi 151. And as if eleven shots of booze weren't enough, we would have "Bomber races": twelve newly 21-year-old jackasses and jackassettes slurping giant red drinks through straws as fast as we could, stopping every so often to cringingly stave off brain freeze. Winning was inconsequential, as we were all shitfaced within eight minutes. I swear, I did go to class in college... and I actually got kind of decent grades.

LIBATION RECOMMENDATION

I thought I would re-create the BJ's Bomber to go with this menu, but then I realized that it sounded like a horrible drink — I guess my tastes have changed a bit in the past decade or so. Instead, I created the Interloper (see recipe, page 202) to lighten things up a bit and to mirror the flavors in the shaved cantaloupe dish.

EFFICIENCY TIP

Do the prep for the dip and the greens first. Then start heating the dip and cooking the broccoli rabe. For the greens, cut the heat after the "5 to 7 minutes of cooking." You can then do the last part of the instructions just before serving. While the greens are cooking and the dip is heating, you can shave the cantaloupe and make the pine nut–basil cream and store them in the fridge. Serve the dip and greens first. When they have been consumed, plate and serve the cantaloupe.

Spinach-Artichoke Dip

3 cups Cashew Ricotta (see recipe, page 95)

1 pound frozen spinach, thawed, water squeezed out, and roughly chopped

One 14-ounce can artichoke hearts, roughly chopped

1 French boule (see WTF below)

2 tablespoons vegan margarine

Assorted fancy-ass breads torn into bite-size pieces for dipping

Salt and pepper

In a medium pot, combine the Cashew Ricotta, spinach, and artichokes, and heat over medium-low heat for 8 to 10 minutes, or until heated through.

Insert a knife into the top of the boule, and cut a wide circular piece as if you were carving the top off of a pumpkin. Remove the "lid" and, with your hands, pull out the bread inside, creating a bread "bowl." Break the chunks of bread that you just extracted from inside the boule into bite-size pieces.

In a large skillet, heat the margarine over medium-high heat. When the margarine is melted, add all the fancy-ass bread pieces. Toast the bread pieces on one side for 2 to 3 minutes, then flip and toast the other side for 2 to 3 more minutes.

Once the dip is warm, season with salt and pepper to taste, and pour it into the bread bowl. Serve it with the toasted bread pieces for dipping.

You'll most likely have extra spinach-artichoke dip. If you and your guests don't eat it all in one sitting, it makes a great filling for pasta shells or lasagna.

WTF is a French boule? It's a round loaf of bread. Well, not completely round; it has a flat bottom. It's more like a dome… yes, a dome of bread that can be made with any type of flour and is perfect for turning into an edible bowl. Most grocery stores carry them.

Braised Broccoli Rabe

1 tablespoon extra-virgin olive oil

2 large shallots, finely chopped

Salt

2 bunches broccoli rabe, roughly chopped

Pepper

2 teaspoons sherry vinegar

1 cup water

1 teaspoon agave nectar

½ cup chopped toasted pecans

In a large skillet, heat the olive oil over medium heat. Add the shallots and a healthy pinch of salt, and cook for 5 to 6 minutes, or until tender. Add the broccoli rabe, another pinch of salt, and a pinch of pepper. Stir until the greens are well coated in the oil, and cook for 2 to 3 minutes. Add the vinegar, water, and agave nectar, cover, and simmer for 5 to 7 minutes, or until the broccoli rabe is wilted and tender. Uncover the skillet, raise the heat to high, and cook for about 3 to 4 minutes, or until the liquid is reduced by half. Remove from the heat, season with salt and pepper to taste, and toss with the pecans.

Shaved Cantaloupe with Pine Nut–Basil Cream

¼ cup pine nuts

1 teaspoon fresh lemon juice

⅛ packed cup fresh basil leaves, plus a few more leaves, very thinly sliced, for garnish

One 1-inch piece banana

2 tablespoons water, plus more as needed

½ cantaloupe, rind and seeds removed, very thinly sliced with a mandoline or sharp knife

Smoked sea salt or regular sea salt, for garnish

Scan to watch the video.

Heat a skillet to medium-high, and toast the pine nuts for 60 to 90 seconds. DO NOT WALK AWAY! They burn fast, so stand by, shaking the pan back and forth until you see them get a little browned. Remove from the heat, and let cool slightly.

In a small food processor or blender, process the pine nuts, lemon juice, ⅛ cup basil, banana, and 2 tablespoons water until smooth. Add more water if the mixture needs to be thinned to a pourable consistency. Layer the cantaloupe slices evenly on a serving plate. Sprinkle a pinch or two of smoked sea salt onto the cantaloupe, drizzle with the pine nut–basil cream, and garnish with sliced basil.

Happy
Hour

Bombers and Bread Bowls

PRODUCE

Banana (1)
Cantaloupe (1)
Lemon (1)
Broccoli rabe (2 bunches)
Garlic (1 clove)
Shallots (2 large)
Basil (1 bunch)

PANTRY

Nutritional yeast (1 heaping tablespoon)
Artichoke hearts (two 14-ounce cans)
Agave nectar (1 teaspoon)
Extra-virgin olive oil (1 tablespoon plus 2 teaspoons)
Sherry vinegar (2 teaspoons)
Cashews, whole raw (2 cups)
Pecans, chopped toasted (½ cup)
Pine nuts (¼ cup)
Smoked sea salt (for garnish; optional)
Salt
Pepper

MISCELLANEOUS

Vegan margarine (2 tablespoons)
Frozen spinach (one 16-ounce bag)
French boule (1)
Assorted breads (for dipping)

20

QUESOME MUCHO

Hatch Chile Queso

Maple-Chipotle Roasted Veggies

Fresh Tomatillo Salad

Shopping List

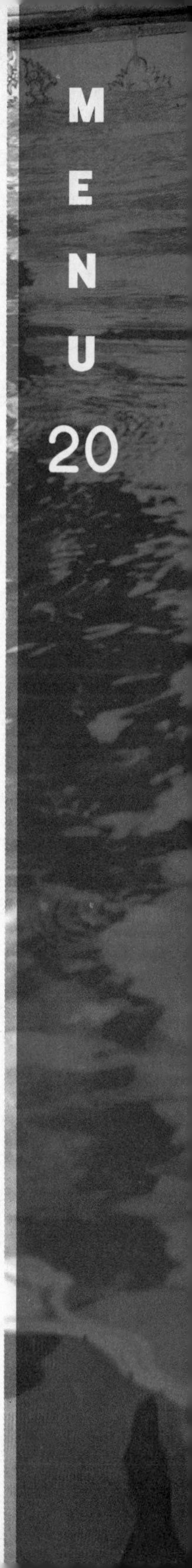

MENU 20

Believe it or not, the state of New Mexico has other exports besides chemically perfect crystal meth. The Hatch chile, born in the town of Hatch, has an almost buttery flavor when roasted and peeled, and the heat can vary from medium to hot. Since its season is very short (mid-August to late-September), you're not always going to be able to get them fresh. You can use canned green chiles (although the dish won't have quite the same awesomeness as when you use fresh) or substitute fresh Anaheim chiles.

LIBATION RECOMMENDATION

The Bloody Vulcan (see recipe, page 193) or Pomarita (see recipe, page 203) would hit the spot with this menu. If you're looking for a blended margarita, might I suggest the Numbskull from my first book? Yes, I might.

EFFICIENCY TIP

First get your chiles roasting, then prep the maple-chipotle veggies and get them in the oven. Next you can brown the Soyrizo while you're blending up the queso. You can cover the roasted veggies with foil to keep them warm or put them in the oven on low. Last, you can prepare the tomatillo salad and the dressing.

Hatch Chile Queso

4 fresh Hatch chiles or two 4-ounce cans diced green chiles

2 teaspoons extra-virgin olive oil

6 ounces Soyrizo or 1½ cups Tempeh Chorizo (recipe follows)

1½ cups whole raw cashews

1 garlic clove

½ teaspoon onion powder

1 cup vegetable stock, plus more as needed

1 teaspoon turmeric

¼ cup nutritional yeast

Salt and pepper

2 Roma tomatoes, seeded and diced

Tortilla chips

Cilantro sprig or sliced scallions, for garnish

If using fresh chiles, you must roast them. Over a medium grill or skillet, roast the fresh chiles, turning occasionally, until blackened on all sides. Place the roasted chiles in a paper bag with the top closed or in a bowl covered with plastic wrap. Let the chiles steam for at least 15 minutes, which further cooks them and makes the skin easier to remove. Remove most of the charred skin and seeds from the chiles. Do not rinse under water, as you'll be rinsing away flavor. Dice the chiles and set aside, reserving 1 tablespoon for the Fresh Tomatillo Salad dressing (see recipe, page 185).

If you're using Soyrizo, in a medium skillet, heat the oil over medium-high heat. Add the Soyrizo, break it up with a wooden spoon, and fry for 3 to 5 minutes, or until browned. Set aside. If you're using Tempeh Chorizo, do not fry it; it is perfect for this recipe as is.

If you don't have a super-duper powerful blender like a Vitamix or Blendtec, you'll need to boil your cashews for about 8 minutes or so, to ensure creaminess. Then, in your blender, combine the cashews, garlic, onion powder, 1 cup vegetable stock, turmeric, nutritional yeast, and 2 tablespoons of the diced chiles, and blend until smooth. Add a little more stock, if necessary, to get a smooth consistency. Season with salt and pepper to taste.

Place the cashew sauce in a small pot over low heat and stir in the remaining chiles and most of the tomatoes and Soyrizo, reserving some tomatoes and Soyrizo for garnish. Cook until heated through. Transfer to a medium crock, garnish with tomatoes, Soyrizo, and a cilantro sprig or scallions. Serve with tortilla chips.

TEMPEH CHORIZO

One 8-ounce package tempeh

4 garlic cloves, grated

1 teaspoon cumin seeds (or ½ teaspoon ground cumin)

¼ teaspoon ground cloves

½ teaspoon ground coriander

1 tablespoon smoked paprika

2 teaspoons dried oregano

2 tablespoons chili powder

Pinch of ground cinnamon

Salt and pepper

2 teaspoons extra-virgin olive oil

1 tablespoon sherry vinegar

1 cup vegetable stock

In a large bowl, combine the tempeh, garlic, cumin, cloves, coriander, paprika, oregano, chili powder, cinnamon, and a pinch of salt and pepper. With a fork, potato masher, or your very clean hands, mash everything together until the tempeh is completely "ground" and coated in the spices.

Heat the olive oil in a large skillet over medium heat, and add the tempeh mixture. Cook for 5 to 7 minutes, or until it gets a bit browned. Add the vinegar and cook for 1 minute, then stir in the vegetable stock. Cover and simmer over medium heat for 4 to 5 more minutes, or until the liquid is almost absorbed. Season with salt and pepper to taste.

You'll end up with about 2 cups of chorizo. If you don't use it all right away, store the excess in an airtight container in the fridge for up to 3 days or in the freezer for up to 1 month.

Maple-Chipotle Roasted Veggies

One 7-ounce can chipotle peppers in adobo sauce

1 tablespoon plus ½ teaspoon extra-virgin olive oil

Juice of ½ lime

2 garlic cloves

1 red bell pepper, cut into 1-inch chunks

1 medium red onion, cut into 1-inch chunks

2 medium zucchini, cut into bite-size chunks

2 medium yellow squash, cut into bite-size chunks

1 tablespoon maple syrup

Salt and pepper

1 ear corn or 1 cup frozen corn kernels, thawed

Preheat the oven to 450°F. Line 2 baking sheets with parchment paper or Silpat baking sheets. In a small food processor or blender, puree the chipotle peppers, their sauce, 1 tablespoon olive oil, the lime juice, and the garlic until smooth.

In a large bowl, combine the bell pepper, onion, zucchini, and yellow squash. Add 2 tablespoons of the chipotle mixture, the maple syrup, and a healthy pinch of salt and pepper, and stir until the vegetables are evenly coated. Spread out the veggies in a single layer on the baking sheets, and put them in the oven. If using fresh corn, coat the ear of corn with the ½ teaspoon of olive oil, and season with salt and pepper. Place the corn on a piece of foil and put that in the oven as well. Roast all the veggies for 20 to 25 minutes, or until browned and tender. If using thawed frozen corn, heat a skillet over high heat with ½ teaspoon oil, and fry for a couple minutes on one side until browned.

Transfer the cooked veggies to a large bowl. When the ear of corn is cool enough to handle, run a knife down the sides of the cob to remove the kernels, and add them to the bowl. Toss to combine, season with salt and pepper to taste, and serve.

Fresh Tomatillo Salad

2 Roma tomatoes, thinly sliced

½ pound tomatillos, husks removed, rinsed, and thinly sliced

Salt and pepper

1 tablespoon diced Hatch chiles, reserved from the Hatch Chile Queso (see recipe, page 180)

¼ cup pepitas (see WTF, page 158)

2 teaspoons fresh lime juice

1 tablespoon extra-virgin olive oil

½ cup water, plus more as needed

1 tablespoon roughly chopped fresh cilantro

Place alternating layers of tomatoes and tomatillos in rows on a serving plate. It should look like they were once standing rows of dominoes and now they're knocked over (I didn't know how else to explain that). Season them with a pinch of salt and a few coarse grinds of pepper. Set aside as you make the dressing.

In a food processor, blend the chiles, pepitas, lime juice, olive oil, water, and cilantro until smooth. If it's not quite pourable, add some more water until it is. Season with salt and pepper to taste. Just before serving, drizzle the dressing over the tomatoes and tomatillos.

SHOPPING LIST

Quesome Mucho

PRODUCE

- Limes (2)
- Roma tomatoes (4)
- Tomatillos (½ pound)
- Hatch chiles (4) or diced green chiles (two 4-ounce cans)
- Red bell pepper (1)
- Zucchini (2)
- Yellow squash (2)
- Corn (1 ear) or frozen corn kernels (1 cup)
- Red onion (1 medium)
- Garlic (3 cloves)
- Cilantro (1 bunch)

PANTRY

- Nutritional yeast (¼ cup)
- Chipotle peppers in adobo sauce (one 7-ounce can)
- Vegetable stock (8 fluid ounces [1 cup], plus more as needed)
- Maple syrup (1 tablespoon)
- Extra-virgin olive oil (about 3 tablespoons)
- Cashews, whole raw (1½ cups)
- Pepitas (¼ cup)
- Onion powder (½ teaspoon)
- Turmeric (1 teaspoon)
- Salt
- Pepper

MISCELLANEOUS

- Tortilla chips for dipping
- Soyrizo (6 ounces) — OR if you want to make my Tempeh Chorizo, you'll need:
  - Garlic (4 cloves)
  - Vegetable stock (8 fluid ounces [1 cup])
  - Extra-virgin olive oil (2 teaspoons)
  - Sherry vinegar (1 tablespoon)
  - Chili powder (2 tablespoons)
  - Ground cinnamon (just a pinch)
  - Ground cloves (¼ teaspoon)
  - Ground coriander (½ teaspoon)

Cumin seeds (1 teaspoon) or ground cumin (½ teaspoon)
Dried oregano (2 teaspoons)
Smoked paprika (1 tablespoon)
Tempeh (one 8-ounce package)

THE COCKTAILS

The Punchy Pineapple

The Bloody Vulcan

Figgy Lifting Drink

Nashitini

The Mangled Mango

Burn Relief

The Starburst

The Interloper

The Pomarita

Solid Gold

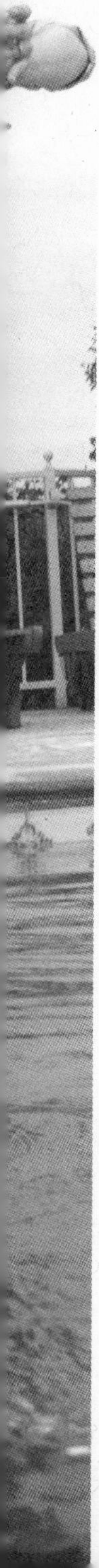

Hey, do you guys remember how in my first book I put the cocktail chapter first and said that cocktails were "the most important meal of the day"? That was pretty funny, huh? Yeah, I'm funny like that. But that was such a long time ago — like thirteen months or something — and I've matured a lot since then. So now I take care of business first, and then kick back with my libations.

I created these cocktails to accompany the menus in this book, but you can have them at other times too. I'm not some cocktail Nazi who says that you can only have cocktails here or there. Have them whenever! Wherever! Whip up a Burn Relief or an Interloper for sipping on the patio on a hot summer night. Or hook up a big batch of Starburst to sneak onto the beach or into the park for a little day drinking. Or, if you're like me, mix up some Bloody Vulcans and have a *Star Trek* marathon on your iPad in the other room, while your wife watches *Gossip Girl* on the big TV. Please enjoy my cocktail creations, and remember to always drink responsibly — meaning, to keep one responsible friend in your group who will drive you around, lie to your wife, and make sure you don't die. You don't even have to like that friend; just make sure you have one.

In order to maximize your spirit-slinging, libation-lobbing, potable-producing enjoyment,

it would be helpful to start off with a few tips about equipment and technique.

Some things that you'll want to have behind your bar:

- a shaker with a strainer top
- a 16-ounce mixing glass
- a 1½-fluid-ounce jigger
- a long-handled bar spoon for stirring
- a muddler (although the handle of a wooden spoon will work in a pinch for mashing fruit and herbs at the bottom of a glass)

And since our days of drinking wine out of big red cups are behind us (mostly), you'll want a variety of glasses to make the drinks look extra-fancy: collins, highball, and martini glasses, as well as tumblers, pilsners, wine glasses, and champagne flutes, should all be in your arsenal.

When it comes to shaking a cocktail, don't wuss out! You gotta shake the crap out of that drink to do it right. Shake your cocktails hard as you count to ten slowly. This will ensure maximum mixage and chillage.

But what about stirring? A cocktail is usually stirred when it comprises only spirits and no other juices or mixers. In those cases (which aren't really in this book), the cocktail is stirred with ice for 60 seconds and then strained. This thoroughly chills and properly dilutes the spirits without leaving little ice shavings in the drink (which some people, like James Bond, enjoy). In the case of the recipes in this book, however, the beverages that are stirred need only be agitated for 10 seconds or so — just enough to chill and mix the ingredients.

Okay, let's get this booze cruise sailing!

The Punchy Pineapple

Seek out some good ginger beer for this cocktail. Your standard grocery store ginger ale just isn't gingery enough. Ginger beer is brewed and has a powerful ginger flavor, whereas ginger ale, as we know it today, is flavored carbonated water with only mild ginger flavor.

Makes 1 cocktail

Ice cubes

2 fluid ounces (1⅓ shots) spiced rum

3 fluid ounces coconut water

2 fluid ounces pineapple juice

3 fluid ounces ginger beer

Splash of Amaretto

Fill a tumbler halfway with ice cubes. Add the rum, coconut water, pineapple juice, ginger beer, and Amaretto. Stir with a long spoon.

The Bloody Vulcan

Tomatoes are red, tomatillos are green, drink several of these, and up you'll be beamed. That was just a sneak preview of my *Star Trek*–themed food poetry book. It's a very niche market.

Makes 1 cocktail

¼ pound tomatillos, quartered

Ice cubes

1½ fluid ounces (1 shot) tequila blanco

1 teaspoon fresh lime juice

1 teaspoon agave nectar

1 jalapeño slice, with a slit so it can sit on the rim of the glass

1 tomatillo slice, with a slit so it can sit on the rim of the glass

To extract the tomatillo juice, run the ¼ pound tomatillos through your juicer or puree them in a food processor or blender. If using a food processor of blender, pass the liquid through cheesecloth to separate the pulp from the juice. You should have about 4 fluid ounces of tomatillo juice.

Fill a collins glass halfway with ice cubes. Add the tequila, tomatillo juice, lime juice, and agave nectar. Stir with a long spoon. Garnish with the jalapeño slice and the tomatillo slice.

Figgy Lifting Drink

In all my genius, I hypothesized that if kombucha helps you digest better and absorb nutrients more effectively, then adding it to a cocktail would get you drunk faster. Since I'm not a scientist (anymore), I didn't really test this hypothesis effectively and have no empirical data to present… but I did get a pretty tasty drink out of it.

Makes 4 cocktails

4 Black Mission figs, quartered lengthwise

6 fluid ounces (4 shots) gin

1½ fluid ounces (1 shot) dry vermouth

4 teaspoons agave nectar

Ice cubes

8 fluid ounces hibiscus kombucha

Chill four martini glasses (see HTF below). Cut a small slit in the bottom of four of the fig pieces, and set them aside. In a mixing glass, combine the gin, vermouth, agave nectar, and remaining fig pieces. Mash these ingredients with a muddler. Add a handful of ice cubes and the kombucha. With a long spoon, stir well. Strain into the chilled martini glasses, and place a fig piece on the rim of each glass.

HTF do I chill martini glasses? Place a few ice cubes in each glass and fill it with water. Set the glasses aside while you prepare the cocktails. When you're ready to pour, discard the ice water from the chilled glasses, shake them out to get rid of most of the excess water (having a bit of water lining the glass is okay), then pour or strain your cocktails into them.

Nashitini

The nashi pear is also known as an Asian pear, Korean pear, Chinese pear, Japanese pear, or apple pear. It has a crisp, grainy texture, and the juice has a light, refreshing flavor. Do not juice the pears more than 10 minutes before making the cocktails because the juice oxidizes very quickly and you'd end up with a brown drink.

Makes 4 cocktails

2 nashi pears, cored
6 fluid ounces (4 shots) sake
1 teaspoon fresh lime juice
1 teaspoon agave nectar
Ice cubes

Chill four martini glasses (see HTF, page 194). To extract the pear juice, run the pears through your juicer or puree them in a food processor or blender. If using a food processor or blender, strain the juice through cheesecloth to remove the pulp. You should have about 8 fluid ounces of pear juice.

In a mixing glass, combine the sake, pear juice, lime juice, agave nectar, and a handful of ice cubes. Stir with a long spoon. Strain your cocktails into the chilled martini glasses.

The Mangled Mango

If you can't get fresh mangoes to puree for this cocktail, you can use the frozen chunks from the freezer section. Just let them thaw before you whip them up.

Makes 1 cocktail

Ice cubes
1½ fluid ounces (1 shot) spiced rum
3 tablespoons mango puree
4 fluid ounces ginger beer
1 lime wedge

Fill a tumbler halfway with ice cubes. Add the rum, mango puree, and ginger beer. Squeeze in the juice from the lime wedge and drop the wedge into the drink. Stir with a long spoon.

Burn Relief

Um, yeah…aloe vera juice…kinda weird, but kinda good. In this drink, I think it's kinda awesome! Try to find the juice without aloe chunks or pulp, but if you can't find it, just strain the chunks or pulp out. I imagine you could have figured that out, but I must be thorough.

Makes 4 cocktails

6 fluid ounces (4 shots) gin
6 fluid ounces aloe vera juice
8 fluid ounces grapefruit juice
2 dashes of Angostura bitters
Ice cubes

Chill four martini glasses (see HTF, page 194). In a shaker, combine the gin, aloe vera juice, grapefruit juice, bitters, and a handful of ice cubes. Shake vigorously for 10 seconds. Strain into the chilled martini glasses.

The Starburst

This is a cocktail I invented in college. It was originally made from V8 Splash, 7 Up, and berry-flavored vodka. Its sugary goodness was a great balance to my savory one-stromboli-a-day meal plan. My roommates and I made it often as a little preparty cocktail before we had to endure whatever horrible "Ice" beer was on sale that night. The only problem was, we had trouble naming it.

Then, late one night, I was zoned out in front of the TV watching bootleg Pearl Jam concert videos and decided to whip one up. Perhaps Eddie Vedder's baritone activated some previously dormant part of my brain, but I took one sip and it hit me: "Starburst! This tastes like a Starburst!" I was so excited that I had finally named our favorite cocktail that I had to wake everyone up and inform them of my revelation. Fortunately they were passed out on the couch next to me with N64 controllers in their hands, so I didn't actually have to get up. Everyone rejoiced. This is a much more healthful and tastier version of that classic beverage.

Makes 1 cocktail

Ice cubes

1½ fluid ounces (1 shot) strawberry vodka

2 fluid ounces fresh carrot juice

2 fluid ounces fresh orange juice

Splash of pineapple juice

1 teaspoon agave nectar

2 fluid ounces club soda

1 lemon wedge

1 lime wedge

Fill a tumbler halfway with ice cubes. Add the vodka, carrot juice, orange juice, pineapple juice, agave nectar, and club soda. Squeeze in the juice from the lemon and lime wedges and drop the wedges into the drink. Stir with a long spoon.

The Interloper

The Interloper is a perfect summer drink. You could try mixing this one up a bit by using honeydew or another melon. Also try basil or even tarragon in place of, or in addition to, the mint. There are endless possibilities for this one.

Makes 1 cocktail

Ice cubes
1½ fluid ounces (1 shot) gin
2 fluid ounces Cantaloupe-Mint Puree (recipe follows)
1 teaspoon agave nectar
4 fluid ounces club soda
1 lime wedge

Fill a tumbler halfway with ice cubes. Add the gin, Cantaloupe-Mint Puree, agave nectar, and club soda. Squeeze in the juice from the lime wedge and drop the wedge into the drink. Stir with a long spoon.

CANTALOUPE-MINT PUREE

¼ average-size cantaloupe, rind and seeds removed, roughly chopped
6 mint leaves

In a food processor or blender, puree the cantaloupe and mint until smooth. This makes about 8 fluid ounces, or enough for 4 cocktails.

The Pomarita

Several years ago, someone gifted me a big, nicely bound, hardcover, journal-type notebook. They said it was for my lyrics. If I remember correctly, I think there was a time, right when I moved to L.A., that I thought I was going to be some kind of songwriter...so everyone just kind of went with that and bought me gifts as if that's what I was. Eventually I realized that I was horrible at all aspects of being a songwriter — playing instruments, singing, and writing songs — so I never wrote a single lyric in that book. The first thing I did write in it, however, was a recipe for a pomegranate margarita. Here's an updated version.

Makes 1 cocktail

Sea salt for the glass (optional)
Lime wedge for the glass (optional)
Ice cubes
1½ fluid ounces (1 shot) tequila oro
2 tablespoons fresh orange juice
2 tablespoons fresh lime juice
½ teaspoon pomegranate concentrate
2 teaspoons agave nectar

On a saucer, spread out the salt in a thin layer. Salt the rim of a tumbler by rubbing the rim with the lime wedge and dipping it in the salt. Fill the tumbler halfway with ice cubes. Add the tequila, orange juice, lime juice, pomegranate concentrate, and agave nectar. Stir with a long spoon.

Solid Gold

You will definitely need a juicer to juice your golden beets. So if you don't have one, go get one. I highly recommend you get yourself a masticating juicer. While they are more expensive, they get more juice out of your veggies, have much better nutrient retention, and are about 8 billion times faster and easier to clean than a centrifugal juicer.

I had a centrifugal juicer once, and it was such a pain in the ass to clean that I hardly ever used it. Now that I have a masticating juicer, I use it almost every day. Once you do a little research on the two types, you'll see the clear winner. Whew! Now that you've done all that researching, learning, and purchasing of a masticating juicer, you deserve a drink. How about this one?

Makes 4 cocktails

¾ pound golden beets
8 fluid ounces fresh orange juice
Ice cubes
6 fluid ounces (4 shots) vodka

Chill 4 martini glasses (see HTF, page 194). Thoroughly wash the beets, and trim off the roots. Cut the beets into manageable pieces and pass them through your juicer. You should have about 4 fluid ounces of beet juice.

As soon as you juice the beets, in a shaker combine the beet juice with the orange juice and stir. This will stop the beet juice from oxidizing and turning brown.

Add a handful of ice cubes and the vodka to the beet–orange juice mixture. Shake vigorously for 10 seconds, and strain into the chilled martini glasses.

Acknowledgments

I WOULD FIRST LIKE TO THANK my beloved New World Librarians for making this yet another fun and smooth book-producing process. To Kristen Cashman and Jane Tunks, who toiled over my every errant word and dangling participle, and to Tracy Cunningham for another super-sexy interior and cover design: thanks for making me sound intelligent and look presentable...I know it's a challenge. On behalf of publicist Kim Corbin, I'd like to apologize to the vegan community and the general public because it's her fault that you're sick of my stupid face and soothing voice. She's just too good at what she does! Really, all of this is Special Sales Manager Ami Parkerson's fault because she was all like, "Hey, New World Library bosses, look at these videos of this vegan guy I found on the Internet — maybe we want to work with him," so you can blame her...I certainly do. Finally, a giant-size mega-thank-you to Editorial Director Georgia Hughes, and all the New World Library chief muckety-mucks, for having faith enough in me to do this again. It is sincerely a pleasure to know and work with you.

Next I'd like to thank the great Dan Boissy, musician, photographer, and Vegin' Out owner extraordinaire. It took me so long to get around to giving you a copy of the first book, and then when I gave it to you, I didn't even write anything in it because I see you all the time and didn't want to have one of those awkward "bro moments." So I'm doing you one better and putting my thanks in print. Thank you for trusting in me to provide healthy, tasty vegan grub to your clients for all these years. I would not be where I am without the opportunity that you have provided me. But most importantly, I'd like to say, "Thank you for being a friend. Da, dum, da, dee, dee, dee, dee." See? Here I am referencing the *Golden Girls* theme song. I couldn't even have a special moment in print. Maybe next time, bro.

Finally, I would like to extend my thanks, love, and adoration to the Wife. Yup, that's right! She stuck it out through "the Girlfriend" and "the Fiancée" portions and is now, miraculously, "the Wife." It was her enthusiasm for these happy hours that led me to put it all in a book. She's my muse, my light, and my compulsive salt-adder. I frigging season things right, but she always has to add a little more — right in front of me, no less! Could be worse...she could put ketchup on everything...in which case I'd be jumping off that balcony. Ahh, marriage. Seriously, I love you, babe. I couldn't imagine a better way to spend eternity.

Even more finally, I would like to thank my unconditionally loving doggies, Chloe and Lucy! Just watching you do the things you do brings unmeasurable joy to our lives. Plus, I always get way more views when you girls show up in my videos, so thank you for that. Also, congratulations on being the first dogs ever to live to over 100 human years old. I'm so glad you'll be with us for our entire lives.

And most finally, I would like to thank the human fetal unit currently floating in the Wife's uterus (I think that's where it is...or is it a womb? I don't know about these things). Thank you so much for being a good kid, and not causing any problems, and not ever keeping us up at night, and not vomiting, pooping, or peeing on us even once. You're the best! One day you'll read this and think, "Man, my dad is a jackass." See you soon, kiddo!

URLs for Accompanying Videos

In case for some reason you don't possess the ability to scan the QR codes in this book — like maybe you only have a dumbphone instead of a smartphone, or you prefer to use one of those old-fashioned computer thingys to surf the Interwebs instead of using a tablet — I have been gracious enough to supply the URLs for each of the videos that accompany this book. What a "man of the people" I am!

Page 11, Stromboli: **http://youtu.be/S96pgK_qOek**

Page 29, Pretend Italian Sausages: **http://youtu.be/aukyfydaUfg**

Page 57, BBQ Jackfruit: **http://youtu.be/6ep4n8oueTI**

Page 79, Stuffed Dates: **http://youtu.be/EtKLOs6N6uo**

Page 94, Rigatoni Poppers: **http://youtu.be/z10W3YiCQno**

Page 105, Tempeh Bacon: **http://youtu.be/PUlgDoDTH3M**

Page 129, U-NO-gi Nigiri with Kabayaki Sauce:
http://youtu.be/7fboJPgWLWk

Page 175, Shaved Cantaloupe with Pine Nut–Basil Cream:
http://youtu.be/WRCbdGH5_9I

Index

For entries in which there is more than one page reference, references in **blue type** indicate the original recipe; references in normal type indicate places where the item is mentioned or used as an ingredient.

About the Author

BRIAN L. PATTON is the executive chef for Vegin' Out, Los Angeles's premier vegan meal delivery service. This quintessential "regular dude" started posting instructional vegan cooking videos on YouTube as his witty, ukulele-playing alter ego "The Sexy Vegan" and quickly gained a large following. In addition to authoring *The Sexy Vegan Cookbook: Extraordinary Food from an Ordinary Dude* and *The Sexy Vegan's Happy Hour at Home*, Brian has been featured in the *New York Times* and the *Huffington Post* and has garnered much praise from *VegNews* magazine, Vegan.com, and countless others in the vegan community. He offers raucous cooking demonstrations at stores, restaurants, and conferences; on television throughout Southern California; and in his travels around the country.

www.thesexyvegan.com

NEW WORLD LIBRARY is dedicated to publishing books and other media that inspire and challenge us to improve the quality of our lives and the world.

We are a socially and environmentally aware company, and we strive to embody the ideals presented in our publications. We recognize that we have an ethical responsibility to our customers, our staff members, and our planet.

We serve our customers by creating the finest publications possible on personal growth, creativity, spirituality, wellness, and other areas of emerging importance. We serve New World Library employees with generous benefits, significant profit sharing, and constant encouragement to pursue their most expansive dreams.

As a member of the Green Press Initiative, we print an increasing number of books with soy-based ink on 100 percent postconsumer-waste recycled paper. Also, we power our offices with solar energy and contribute to nonprofit organizations working to make the world a better place for us all.

Our products are available
in bookstores everywhere.
For our catalog, please contact:

New World Library
14 Pamaron Way
Novato, California 94949

Phone: 415-884-2100 or 800-972-6657
Catalog requests: Ext. 50
Orders: Ext. 52
Fax: 415-884-2199
Email: escort@newworldlibrary.com

To subscribe to our electronic newsletter, visit:
www.newworldlibrary.com

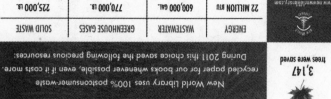

HELPING TO PRESERVE OUR ENVIRONMENT

New World Library uses 100% postconsumer-waste recycled paper for our books whenever possible, even if it costs more. During 2011 this choice saved the following precious resources:

3,147 trees were saved

ENERGY	WASTEWATER	GREENHOUSE GASES	SOLID WASTE
22 MILLION BTU	600,000 GAL.	770,000 LB.	225,000 LB.

www.newworldlibrary.com

Environmental impact estimates were made using the Environmental Defense Fund Paper Calculator @ www.papercalculator.org.